Island of Truth

BY THE SAME AUTHOR

REBUILDING SHAHJAHANABAD
The Walled City of Delhi (Vikas Publishing House Pvt Ltd)

Island of Truth

JAGMOHAN

VIKAS PUBLISHING HOUSE PVT LTD
New Delhi Bombay Bangalore Calcutta Kanpur

VIKAS PUBLISHING HOUSE PVT LTD
5 Ansari Road, New Delhi 110002
Savoy Chambers, 5 Wallace Street, Bombay 400001
10 First Main Road, Gandhi Nagar, Bangalore 560009
8/1-B Chowringhee Lane, Calcutta 700016
80 Canning Road, Kanpur 208004

COPYRIGHT © JAGMOHAN, 1978

ISBN 0 7069 0660 8

1V02J0303

Printed at Dhawan Printing Works, 26-A Mayapuri, New Delhi 110064

To
all those but for whose persistent efforts to denigrate, to mislead, and to hide the underlying truth, this book would never have been written

There are many who dislike me
Blaming for this and that....
Their jealous look of malice
I feel behind my back.

But I am pleased with all this,
And I am proud because
They cannot break me down
And make me leave my cause.

ACKNOWLEDGEMENTS

I would like to express my gratitude to my younger brother, Dr P.L. Malhotra, for going through the manuscript of this book and making valuable suggestions. I am also indebted to my wife, Uma, and my two children, Deepika and Mohan, whose willingness to suffer for the cause of truth has been a source of great inspiration to me.

Thanks are also due to my friends and staff of Sapru House Library whose attitude of cooperation has not changed when most other things around seem to be changing.

PREFACE

Delhi and its historicity has always fascinated me. Here, every stone sings the story of bygone ages. The air we breathe has the dust and fragrance of the past, hope and despair of the present, and challenges and opportunities of the future. From Inderprastha, the legendary Delhi of Pandavas, to the Ninth Delhi—the Delhi of Naraina and Vikaspuri, of Dakshanpuri and Tirlokpuri, of Yamuna River Front and Tughlakabad city forest, of 16 lakh new trees and hundreds of woodlands and parks, of Nehru Place and Vikas Minar, of Okhla industries and new markets and terminals—there is one vast spectacle of history which enthrals as well as depresses, charms as well as repels. The epic drama unfolds scene after scene, of triumph and tragedy, of love and hatred, of rise and fall. The book describes one such scene—the scene of the emergency period in which I also participated.

During my long association with Delhi's development, I came in contact with people from all walks of life—from slum-dwellers to the Prime Minister, from squatters, who showed me their wounds with the zest of a beggar, to the heartless racketeers, who operated behind the scene in the name of human considerations. I had also the opportunity to work with magnanimous officers who passed on to me the credit which was really theirs, as well as with the jealous bureaucrats whose sole preoccupation was to cut the ground underneath my feet. I had the fortune of securing the highest form of loyalty from my colleagues and also the misfortune of being stabbed in the back by those who once swore by my name. All this has provided me some insight into the inner layers of Indian society and also taught me to take triumphs and tribulations with stoic calm.

Even a short sojourn on my island of truth will reveal the extent to which a false picture has been painted and our people and persons in authority kept in dark about the reality.

How many of us have been told that before the operation resettlement the squatters were scattered on road berms, slushy and stinking beds of the river and embankment of *nallahas* etc., in 1,400 haphazard clusters, 72 per cent of which had no water taps, 69 per cent no lavatories, 68 per cent no storm water drain and 63 per cent no street lighting? How many of us have been told that in one year, about 2,000 acres of developed land, the market value of which exceeds Rs 200 crores, has been distributed amongst the urban poor, and that this is the biggest socialist measure ever taken in the city of any developing country in the world?

And what about the much-maligned Turkman Gate incident? Is it not shocking that none of the writers of the Turkman Gate story makes it clear that the area had been declared unfit for human habitation, that the houses in question had been acquired, that, as was tragically demonstrated by eight subsequent deaths due to collapse of houses, the inmates lived under constant risk of death, and that, against 120 houses cleared, about 1,000 alternative allotments had been made, including 200 flats in the most attractive colony of Ranjit Nagar/Patel Nagar and 200 commercial plots? Why no one speaks of the compensation, of beautiful flats, or of liberal terms of allotment of plots and commercial sites, the market value of which would run into several lakhs? Why everyone speaks of bulldozers knowing that they were used, as in the last decade or so, for clearing the debris?

When the autumn is gone, the storm blown over, and the dust and haze of ignorance and prejudice settled down, the true faces of those guilty of falsifying history will stand exposed. Today, by their own queer logic of slant and slander, they may paint a false picture. But what will be the verdict of history? How will they escape the terrible consequences of their falsehood? Will not their murky soul stifle and destroy them? Truth can be hid, but not for all times.

Truth annoys power, because it is stronger than power and it takes time to demonstrate its strength. More often than not persons with good intentions have been overwhelmed by the forces of their time. The more attached they are to the basic truth, the worse are they likely to be treated by their compatriots. As Trotsky once observed, the modern tragedy, in essence, lies in the wider conflict between man's awakened mind and his constricting environment.

The book is in the form of an address to the Shah Commission. It is largely based upon what I stated before the Commission and what I submitted it in writing, but which was never published. The book presents the context and the wider perspective of the problem. It explains what was done in the pre-emergency days, and how various interests are now picking up wrong end of the stick, and confusing development with destruction, justice with technicality, dynamism with ruthlessness, humanism with brutality. It also exposes lies, half-truths and convenient conscience and the inner disease that afflicts us all. Finally, the book unfolds the untold story of Turkman Gate, and provides glimpses of the Ninth Delhi, that is, Delhi developed by the Delhi Development Authority during the last ten or fifteen years.

The book has been written from a roadside shelter in which I have taken temporary refuge during the current torrential rain. I seek forgiveness if a drop or two has leaked from my shelter and drenched a few of my papers. Truth, moreover, by its very nature is not tactful and has no tactics.

JAGMOHAN

CONTENTS

Chapter I
ISLAND OF TRUTH   1

Chapter II
THE CONTEXT   19

Chapter III
BACKGROUND AND THE PRE-EMERGENCY DAYS   26

Chapter IV
THE EMERGENCY DAYS   45

Chapter V
DEMOLITION OR DEVELOPMENT?   57

Chapter VI
LIES, HALF-TRUTHS AND CONVENIENT CONSCIENCE   77

Chapter VII
THE DISEASE THAT AFFLICTS US ALL   95

Chapter VIII
UNTOLD STORY OF TURKMAN GATE   121

Chapter IX
NINTH DELHI   170

Epilogue   188

Notes   191

Appendixes   193

Index   203

CHAPTER I

ISLAND OF TRUTH

> And the truth cannot be hid
> Somebody chose their pain
> What need not have happened did.
>
> AUDEN

Mine is an island of truth—truth in its essence, truth in its basic framework. I intend to take you to this island. But for reaching this island, we have to pass through a turbulent sea of falsehood. The island, too, is desolate and deserted. Of late, it has been visited by marauders and systematically pillaged and shorn of its greenery. The sentinels themselves have been terrorized. They are silent:

> That silence roars on my behalf
> Silence tear my ears
> All know it and are silent
> Their mouths are stifled by fear.

Notwithstanding the silence and sulleness that has gripped this once buoyant and thriving island, I hope to show you a few spots from which the reality may emerge, and you may be able to see true reflections even in a cracked mirror. You may realize that what was done in Delhi during the emergency was development and not "demolition." It was a dawn, not a doom.

Politics and struggle for power should not concern us. But can we ignore their all pervasive influence? The grime and filth of politics has, unfortunately, invaded every aspect of our activity, and even the remotest corner of civic sphere has not been spared. It will be a mistake to confine ourselves to the surface only and not to peep into the underlying reality. If you look at the outward manifestation of what is really an inner disease, you are likely to arrive at erroneous conclusions. These may merely result in diverting the attention of the people from the real to the superficial causes and impel them to make graver and graver mistakes and go deeper and deeper into the grime and filth of politics.

In the chaos of struggle for power and spiritual malaise, the surgeon becomes the butcher and it is the darker instincts of man that get an upper hand. Lies, slander and suspicion seep into his mental framework, and make him a slave of his prejudices and notions. What else could be the explanation for all the lies that have been spoken with impunity—lies by a section of the press and writers, lies by persons in authority, lies by public servants, and lies by some people who are willing to be tutored, and perjure themselves.

Immediately after the termination of the emergency, a special brand of press reports and books started appearing. They churned out stories of atrocities. These stories—so far as they relate to demolition/clearance by the Delhi Development Authority—were either concoctions or products of prejudiced and superficial minds. Even elementary care in checking facts and backgronnd of policy and programme was not taken. Regard for truth and basic human values, the suppression of which during the emergency was condemned, was crucified. It shows what little commitment to these values really exist.

Patently false stories were circulated. If anyone offered to indicate the correct facts, the offer was contemptuously spurned. No prick of conscience was felt in coining stories or picking up rumours and publishing them as inside accounts, right from the horse's mouth. Going through such stories, designed both to collect easy money and inflict mental pain—reprehensible objectives by any standard—I often wondered whether, in a diseased society, freedom of expression did not really amount to freedom to speak lies. All institutions and components of power structure in our country may have the same framework, the same legal and constitutional basis, as in other healthy democratic societies of the West. But what is different is the spirit, the motivation, with which these institutions and components of power structure are run. Because of the current hold of hypocrisy and superficiality on our society, the cause of truth and justice is not well served by the components of power structure like the fourth estate. Let me give an example.

In the *Indian Express* (19 April 1977) a story appeared on its front page about the Turkman Gate clearance. The main thrust of the story, so far as it related to the Delhi Development Authority, was that on 18 April 1976, Sanjay Gandhi, two unidentified women and myself were sitting in Ranjit Hotel when some persons including one Kayam-u-din came to see us. They begged us to stop the demolition/clearance. Sanjay, so the story proceeded, kept quiet but I blurted out, "we do not want second Pakistan."

The story was reprinted in *Seminar* (June 1977). It was published by various other magazines as if the writers had personal knowledge and were present at the time of the alleged confrontation. D.R. Mankekar in his book *Decline and Fall of Indira Gandhi* went a step further. He wrote with the authority of a researcher and an impartial eye-witness.

The story was a sheer fabrication. But its circulation stopped only when an American journalist published an interview in July 1977 with Sanjay Gandhi in which the latter disclosed that on 18 April 1976 he was in Simla with his mother, Indira Gandhi. This disclosure was reproduced in the *Times of India*.

Soon after its publication, I wrote to the *Indian Express:* "Turkman Gate story, published in your paper, so far as it pertains to me, is totally incorrect. For legal and other reasons, however, I would not like to say anything more at this stage." My letter to *Seminar* read:

> Your write-up, so far as it pertains to me, is incorrect and highly defamatory... a sheer concoction, indeed.... I hope you will agree that for a sensitive person there is no greater torture than the mental torture of being subjected to false accusations. Nor can there be any greater injustice to history and public information than the publication of such inaccurate and motivated reports....

I sent similar letters to the editors of the magazines in which this story appeared. What did the apostles of freedom of expression do? They did not even acknowledge my letters, what to speak of publishing them. The crisis from which we are suffering is far more serious than what it appears at the surface. It has penetrated deep into the soul of the nation. It was certainly not confined to those who caused the emergency or were drawn into its orbit.

What some ex-ministers and persons in authority said before the Shah Commission is still more shocking. They suppressed the truth to project an image of purity for themselves and what was worse, to accuse others by making it appear that the blame was entirely theirs.

For instance, after approving and answering a number of questions in Parliament on demolition/clearances and resettlement, after presiding over the meetings of the Parliamentary Consultative Committee in which the issue was repeatedly discussed, after visiting the resettlement colonies, and after getting the slum and squatter settlements in the rear of his bungalow cleared, K. Raghuramiah, former Minister of Works, Housing and Parliamentary Affairs, told the Commission, in reply to its questions, that he was hearing for the first time about the slum and squatter clearance and resettlement programme. By implications, he wanted to convince the Commission that others were carrying out the programme against his wishes.

The Commission must have noted that Raghuramiah, otherwise an extremely amiable, upright and a lovable personality with sparkling wit and mental alertness, was not the only one to adopt this posture. Some other persons in authority did the same. Their stand during the emergency and subsequent deposition before the Commission reflect a crisis of value, a crisis of national character. It is futile to find fault with the individuals. They only represent the crisis. And will not history or the Commission pose a number of basic questions to these persons in authority: Why did they not resign when either their subordinates or their superiors ignored them? Why were they willing to support the same power structure after the elections? Would they have been terrorized if they had not sought election tickets, asked for votes in the name of the old set-up, and tried to become ministers again?

What about public servants? Why are they feigning ignorance and speaking lies? Apart from the general malaise and crisis of character, which has badly affected the morale and outlook of public services, the attitude of most public servants who deposed before the Commission appears to have been influenced by other considerations.

The officers who are now blaming others neither cared to understand the background policy of clearance and resettlement, nor assessed its intrinsic worth. They were more attuned to obeying orders to seek advancement. They never argued their case or asserted their viewpoint. Now, they find it hard to muster facts to justify what they did. Fear of Maintenance of Internal Security Act has naturally become a convenient alibi for them.

One may, to some extent, believe that there were risks involved in disobeying authority. But would the officers have been put behind bars if they had not held daily press conferences or regularly appeared before the television, as was done by Kishan Chand, former Lieutenant Governor, and B.R. Tamta, former Municipal Commissioner, to sing songs in praise of the programmes and policies of the day? In fact, it were officers like Kishan Chand and Tamta who set new norms of behaviour and made it embarrassingly difficult for the conscientious officers to stand up to some odd features of the new situation.

Another factor which played a significant part in making the public servants say what they said was the policy announcement of the Commission. On quite a few occasions, the Commission made it clear that it would not recommend action against those who merely carried out the orders and who were willing to point to the source from which the orders emanated. This statement was seized by the weaker, the indolent, and the casual element in the public services to cover their own commissions and procedural lapses. The subordinate officers are now only too eager to make their seniors, who are defending their actions, a scapegoat, particularly when a prejudice has been built around them by propaganda, publicity in the press, and hostility of some elements in the power structure.

"He lies like an eye witness," says a Russian proverb. Most witnesses drawn from public, such as those from Turkman Gate area, were tutored. Siraj Piracha and Inder Mohan, who go about as social workers, were seen prompting them openly. When, for instance, Mrs Anaro started blurting out her tutored version, she, in the heat of the moment, forgot to say something about which she had been told. Someone shouted from the audience—Jagmohan's story! Then, the needle went on the "tutored groove of the gramophone" and she spoke in one breath. She said, "while our houses were being pulled down, Sanjay and Jagmohan were drinking at the site." No one asked her where and when this happened, and what time and date it was. No one questioned her about my identification, particularly when she repeatedly spoke about my non-existent office[1] in Jhandewalan and her supposed meeting with me in that office. Thousands of my friends and acquaintances and a large section of Delhi population know that I have not touched any intoxicant all my life. Yet, the bizarre, totally concocted story of Mrs Anaro, was broadcast at 9 P.M. from the national hook-up of the All India Radio. What does this show? Regard for truth and justice? Or respect for value?

What happened on 23 December 1977 at about 4 P.M., when Kayam-u-din was tendering evidence, is equally revealing. After making wild allegations about the Turkman Gate incident, Kayam-u-din said something which P.N. Lekhi, government counsel to the Commission, did not expect him to say. The latter gesticulated nervously to the operators of the tape-recorder and the loudspeaker and the tone of the instruments was lowered (if not switched off temporarily). Thereafter, Lekhi went to the dias of the witness and whispered something to Kayam-u-din who replied rather loudly: "I am not one of those whom you tutor, 'rehearse' and than bring as witness." Then, it was the turn of "social worker" Siraj Piracha to go to the chair immediately behind the dias of the witness and suggest to Kayam-u-din to send his written statement afterwards. Kayam-u-din shouted back, "I would not give any written statement." In such circumstances, will it be safe for the Commission to rely on the oral evidence that is being tendered before it?

What led to the publication of false stories? Why did ex-ministers and persons in authority choose to suppress the truth? Why tutoring of witnesses had to be resorted to?

These are the questions which the Commission may address itself. And these would lead us to larger and more basic questions. Are we not making our liberty an instrument of repression? Has not the creeping paralysis of values affected us from top to bottom?

If this is the reality of the situation, what good would come out of abstract values of law and justice? Technicality of law and procedure may lead you to some conclusion. But will these conclusions be really fair? What about the intrinsic merit, the intrinsic justice? What about the fundamental question of bringing about just and fair system by just and fair means? And what about the illegal builders and land grabbers, who came to the Commission with a tainted conscience? What moral right have they to take advantage of the technical and procedural omissions, when they themselves showed no respect for law and violated all revenue, municipal, and master plan rules and regulations for pecuniary and personal advantage and ravaged this great and historic city with unauthorized constructions and illegal encroachments, exposing the law-abiding citizens to grave hazards of health and traffic safety? Need the Commission go to the peripheral issues alone and not the real ones? Which are the worse excesses—excesses which occur due to technical lapses or excesses which ooze out like an overflowing sewerage from a decaying spiritual framework of the society?

I have all the respect for law and its basic rationality. But the way in which it actually operates in civic sphere is disturbing. In Delhi, it is in the backyards of "temples of justice" that maximum violation of civic laws takes place, and the offenders mostly get away with it, combining political pressures with the delays inherent in the system. I am, let me make it clear, not blaming the courts, but the total legal system and its various components, including the attitude of the litigants. They usually approach the courts not with a view to seeking justice but with a view to buying time during which political strings could be pulled, "human consideration" invoked, and conscientious officers bullied.

The manner in which the legal system has been operating in the civic sphere demonstrates in a classic way that, apart from the importance of the structure of the institutions, it is the spirit with which these institutions are run that really matters. In the absence of proper spirit, the institutions intended to serve a particular cause actually happen to serve exactly the opposite purpose. It is, indeed, "paradoxical to have justice object to such steps as endeavour to bring justice into an unjust situation." The vested interests are able to exploit the system, and this is causing incalculable harm to the city, the people and the rule of law itself.

Is it not fair that this aspect of the case, which carries in its womb the real seed of the so-called excesses, should also be looked into? True dictates of true justice require that underlying reality should be thoroughly probed. Then alone the microbes that cause the disease will be eliminated. Then alone sound foundation for a healthy and lasting superstructure can be laid. Tinkering with the problem or dealing with its outward manifestation would be of no consequence at all to the society as a whole; it may merely harm a few individuals who happened to occupy a particular position at a particular time.

If the basic realities of the situation are not faced and if the basic difficulties are not obviated, the same old procedures and practices, the same old policy and programmes, would continue. It is not for nothing that even now the earlier procedures and policies that are sought to be condemned before the Commission are being followed. From 26 September 1977 to 3 December 1977, 3,675 structures were demolished by the DDA, which gives an average of 245 structures per day. No notice was issued or alternative accommodation provided.

What is the morality, what is the respect for law, which the vote-seeker and the vote-giver generally exhibit in Delhi. The former tells the latter: "If you vote for me, I will have all your illegal acts condoned, and get your unauthorized constructions and encroachments regularized." He is not bothered whether provision for such regularization exist in law or not. Nor is he concerned about the perversion of values, the benefits that would accrue to land racketeers and law breakers and the contempt which his action would generate for law in the common man. He swears by Gandhi on the one hand and encourages contempt for law and morality on the other. Straight-forwardness demands that if our laws are unenforceable against vested interests, it is much better to amend or scrap them. Why are the citizens of Delhi being made dishonest? Why is it being demonstrated that law-breaking pays?

Our critics usually ignore the enormity of the problems which we face. Whatever one may do, they know how to condemn it. They have an easy task of finding faults. Practical realities are none of their concern. They cheat the problem and its mathematics; they spurn statistics. They are not bothered about such basic issues as availability of finance or lands and municipal services or low levels of income of the people, or institutional drawbacks, or difficulties inherent in the social and economic imbalances of our society. They do not care to know that the Delhi Master Plan, by no means an ambitious document, involved a financial outlay of Rs 732 crores at 1962 price level, and that not even one-fourth of this outlay was made available. Nor does it concern them that about 70 per cent of Delhi population, to which about one lakh poor people are being added every year, cannot afford to live in the low-income group housing of the public authorities, and that in the sphere of slum clearance alone, it will take, at the present level of investment, at least twenty-five-year plans to resettle all the slum and shack-dwellers in decent houses.

On the one hand, we have problems of baffling magnitude and complexity, on the other, we have extremely fragile and weak instruments—an administrative set-up sapped by multiplicity of authorities, a legal system capable of being misused, a civic leadership willing to be pressurized, and somewhat indifferent and apathetic people without much respect for the heritage of the past and regard for the future. What has been done in Delhi for its planned development and environmental upgradation is by any standard significant. This achievement assumes glorious dimensions when viewed in the context of the tremendous problems that had to be faced.

"The world was created, not by words, but by deeds." In the performance of these deeds, it is the nature of the motivating force that determines the worth of the deeds performed. What were my motivations, my objectives, my outlook? I have always believed in the destiny of this city, in its historic role, in its being a spiritual workshop of the nation, in its capacity to impart urbanity and civility to the rural migrant, and in its ability to weave the dismembered threads of our national existence into a strong and well-knit fabric. I have always made earnest efforts to make Delhi an ideal city, a model for other cities to follow, a city which should be an organ of love and justice and whose economy should be the care and culture of its men and women. It has not mattered to me whether my efforts have made me unpopular. Unpopularity and opposition of the vested interests are inherent in this approach and for safeguarding the future. If Baron Haussmann, the Prefect of Paris for 17 years from 1850 to 1877, had not cleared the slums of place du carrousel, ill de la city and area around Norte Dame, and not built the great highways, the boulevard St. German, St. Michal, Malesherbes, Magenta, Voltaire, and not planted thousands of trees, Paris would have been today an ugly and despicable town, and not a pride of France, a sick and soulless city, and not a seat of vigorous and vibrant culture. Genuine policy is never a thing of the moment, it is a mean for building a path for the future.

It was in pursuance of this motivation that I waged a relentless campaign to bring about planned and balanced development of Delhi, to evolve a rational and equitable urban land policy, to make available residential plots and houses on a large scale to the low and middle-income groups, to ensure complementary development of industry, commerce, institutions, and public utilities, to upgrade the environment of historical places, to eliminate some of the most abominable slums on the road sides, embankments of stinking drains and slushy beds of the river and *nallahs*, and to resettle the squatters in the newly developed resettlement colonies with basic civic amenities and community facilities.

The campaign was bitter and hard. About 600 writ petitions and suits alone had to be fought. Like a mauled leopard, the vested interests hid themselves behind the bush to pounce upon their victim when the opportunity came their way. I was conscious of the consequences. As far back as 1974, in the Epilogue to my book, *Rebuilding Shahjahanabad: The Walled City of Delhi*, I had almost perdicted the situation in which I find myself today:

> I know
> I am no genius
> No Haussmann reborn
> No Lutyens with a chance
> Or Corbusier with Nehru's arms
> I am a little fellow
> An orphan of these streets
> Learning to cry and crawl
> Along the ditches' stagnant shawl
> Growing by the side of a butcher's shop
> Yet
> With all the millstones
> Around my neck

Island of Truth

> I stand erect
> Restless and keen
> Willing to fight
> Willing to dream
> For a while
> I thought
> In my papers
> In my voiceless sketches
> Warmly drawn
> Lay the hope of a silken dawn
> For this battered child of Shahjahan
> But this sick and soulless city
> Wounds me with its hidden claws
> Beats me with my imaginary flaws
> Shattered shaken
> I stand alone
> With the sheaf of papers all flown.

But I always thought it better to have fought and lost than not to have attempted at all. Even the defeat has not been without its saga of Delhi development. It resulted in the acquisition of about 42,000 acres of urban land, development of over 300,000 residential plots and 40,000 houses, mostly for the urban poor in the low and middle-income groups, setting up of new industrial estates providing developed land for shifting of about 3,500 non-conforming industries from the congested portion of the city, and construction of Asia's biggest Inter-State Bus Terminus at Ring Road, Asia's biggest Cycle Market at Jhandewalan, Asia's biggest new wholesale fruit and vegetable market at Azadpur, and new commercial and business centres like Nehru Place, Rajindra Place providing office and business space four times the space available in Connaught Place. It also led to the creation of scores of city forests and woodlands and plantation of about 1.6 million trees. A small seed capital of about Rs 5 crores was evolved to the extent of about 27 times its original size. New techniques of balancing unremunerative projects against remunerative ones were deviced to secure harmonious development of the capital, to preserve its architectural and cultural heritage, and to ensure healthy environment for future without relying upon the budgetary allocation of the government.

Do the dictates of truth and justice require that today I should be judged not by the contribution I have made to Delhi development, but by a few technical and procedural issues, and by what a particular officer did or did not do?

It was unanimous opinion of the local leader, and representatives of all the leading political parties, expressed through the study group constituted by the central government in 1967, that the size of the plots should be restricted to 25 sq. yds., that the squatters should be moved to the periphery of the city, where only absolutely minimum facilities like drinking water and community latrines should be provided. Why the representatives of some political parties are now criticizing that only 25 sq. yds. of plots have been allotted and the squatters settled at what are considered distant sites? Why, after having solemnly resolved that the problem of squatters will be treated as non-political, nothing but politicalization of the issue has taken place? Why is there such a fundamental difference between the opinion expressed by political parties in the official meetings and their public postures outside?

These questions may not prick our conscience today. But one day we will have to pay a heavy price for this. Evaporation of ethics from our over-heated political system will leave it high and dry. It will crack and collapse by its own excesses, by its internal contradictions and imbalances. The Commission wants to know the truth. Will such a set-up, such an environment, nurse and protect truth?

Regarding slum-dwellers what were our basic objectives, basic intentions? This would be clear from the fact that before clearance-cum-resettlement operations were undertaken on a large scale, there were about 1,400 haphazard, ill-planned, clusters, scattered all over the city in unsuitable and unhealthy sites. Contrary to the general impression, 78 per cent of the squatter households were living beyond 6.5 km of the centre of the city (Connaught Place). About 71.8 per cent of these 1,400 settlements were not having any water taps, 58.31 per cent had no hand-pumps, 68.9 per cent no lavatory seats, 65.1 per cent no brick pavements or pucca streets, 68.9 per cent no storm water drains and 63.1 per cent no street lighting. With extreme congestion and irregular and shapeless structures, with only 4 per cent of pucca shacks, with unstable families and low sex ratio (730 females: 1,000 males), the environmental degradation could not be worse.[2]

It was from these sub-human conditions that the squatters were relieved and accommodated in the 27 resettlement colonies. Extraordinary hard work was put in to provide maximum facilities to the largest number in the shortest time. In about a year or so, about 1,45,000 residential and 10,000 shop plots were developed, and 200 km of main drains, 400 km of small drains, 650 culverts, 60 tubewells, 4,000 hand-pumps, 2,500 public hydrants, 80 km of water supply lines, 200 km of metalled roads, and 14,000 permanent lavatory seats were constructed. About 500 parks were developed, besides planting 5 lakhs trees. Ten new higher secondary school buildings, 23 new dispensaries, 60 TV sheds were also constructed. In some colonies, facilities of supper-bazars, community halls, adult literacy centres, milk-bars, "balbaries," etc., were provided. In addition to the employment opportunities existing in the neighbourhood of the resettlement colonies, a large number of new employment opportunities were provided. During the peak period, about 12,000 persons were employed every day. About 250 trucks, 25 road-rollers, and 20 bulldozers were engaged per day. About 5 lakhs bags of cement and 50,000 truck-loads of bricks were consumed in the development work of the resettlement colonies. As compared to almost cent per cent construction (excepting small lanes) in pre-resettlement sites, the resettlement colonies were planned and developed with only 32 per cent of the area as residential, 13 per cent was earmarked for metalled roads, 15 per cent for paths, 16 per cent for parks, 4 per cent for shops, and 20 per cent for community facilities.

All this shows the tremendous effort put in by the Delhi Development Authority to put the squatters on the road to progress and prosperity. About 1,000 hectares of land was developed with basic environmental and community facilities and allotted on nominal rent. House-building loans from the banks, which were never available before, were arranged. Uptil May 1977, about Rs 8.3 crores had been disbursed to about 65,000 squatter families to construct substantial dwellings on the plots allotted to them. The entire programme was development-oriented, and not "demolition-oriented."

In these circumstances, should I or any of my staff be accused of harshness or ignoring the human considerations? Our intentions, our motives, are reflected in the sincere efforts and hard work put in.

By creating new organized settlements, with sizable population, we have taken advantage of the economies of scale and concentrated on environmental, educational, cultural, and recreational facilities which would improve the quality of mind and help the people in acquiring better social habits. The real problem of slums is not taking people out of slums but slums out of people. Because of the paucity of resources, we cannot provide more space or more houses to slum-dwellers but we can certainly create environment in which human personality is not stifled and the future generation can grow with better influence and become a more productive and healthy unit of the society.

Ours was a pioneering effort and, like any other effort of this nature, would admit improvements in future. The size of the plot allotted to individual family is, undoubtedly, small. But in an administrative set-up, which is extremely conservative in allotting financial resources and which is not fully conscious of the impact of new forces of over-population and over-urbanization, to secure even this meagre allotment is not insignificant. Moreover, in practice, it has been seen that wherever larger space has been allotted, the unit is usually sub-let in part and the original allottee confining himself to a smaller space.

There are social, economic, and financial constraints and a number of impediments arising out of what Galbraith called "conventional wisdom." It will take time to get over them. The pioneering effort has already weakened the prevailing notions. The resettlers are gradually learning to take advantage of using larger space, and public authorities are showing greater awareness of the need to allocate larger resources both in terms of land and money. But these resources would be forthcoming in larger measure if the process of migration is made "development-oriented" and not "service-oriented" and the merits of the planned settlement against haphazard squatting are recognized.

What has been done by us, and this has either escaped the notice of superficial observers or deliberately ignored by our critics and self-styled experts, is that not only residential population has been disbursed but also industries, the commerce, and numerous other avenues of employment. Have not the wholesale fruit and vegetable market, iron merchant market, the "kabari" markets, the spare part machinery market, truck terminals, etc., been shifted to the outlying areas? Are not thousands of new industries, new housing complexes, cattle resettlement farms, and milk dairies fast coming up in these areas? There is an overall development pattern in which our resettlement colonies fit. They do not exist in isolation.

And has any one cared to reply the obvious questions: where are the nearby areas where permanent resettlement of about 1,20,000 squatter families, involving a population of about 700,000, could be carried out? Which are the sites available near the heart of the city—Ramlila Ground, area around Red Fort and samadhis, India Gate or Purana Quilla? Is it not inescapable that in a city whose population comprises 80 per cent poor people and whose structural legacy cannot be got rid of in the forceable future, a sizable portion of the poor should be living in the outlying areas? Would it make any sense to provide services at sites which are needed for roads, bridges, and community facilities or constitute road berms or embankments of drains and railway tracks?

The standard of open spaces in our cities is distressingly low—it is only 0.83 acres per 1000 population against six times that proportion in the American cities and fifteen times for the English lawns. On the other hand, the densities of population in our cities are incredibly high. For instance, in the walled city of Delhi, about half a million people are jampacked in two square miles of area, and localities like Maliwara and Dariba Kalan have the highest congestion rate in the world, with a gross density of 670 persons per acre. By this yardstick, about 2,010 persons should be living in premises where the Commission is holding its deliberations. Can any practical approach ignore these realities? I hope the Commission would agree that "things are not revolutionized by creating resolutions. The real revolution lies in the solution of existing problems."

To what extent our expanding metropolis has been put on the map of the world and how the cityscape had become a matter of national pride, would be evident by the observations made by knowledgeable and eminent persons who visited our development projects in the recent past. In view of the deliberate denigrations to which our development effort has been subjected, it would not be out of place to invite attention to some of these observations. Mrs Margaret Thatcher, Leader of the Conservative Party in Great Britain, in September 1976 said:

> A lot was being done in the field of housing and development in Delhi which was not known to us. It is evident from the excellent work shown to me by Delhi Development Authority which was very much different from what I saw during my last visit. I wish I had more time to see the transformed city. Houses constructed by Delhi Development Authority are simply marvellous. I did not realise you are doing so well here, and so much.

In February 1976, President of the Royal Town Planning Institute, London, remarked: "It is wonderful to see that the Delhi Development Authority has so much vision and its officers have so much enthusiasm." Mrs Jill Foot, wife of Michael Foot, Leader of the House of Commons, Great Britain, observed:

> How encouraging to discover modern town planning and housing projects. Others have much to learn from Delhi planning. The public housing and urban village development programme of Delhi Development Authority is the best seen so far in any country.

And this is what Mrs Gabrielle Kibble, daughter of the Governor General of Australia, herself an architect and environmentalist, had to say: "We have a great deal to learn from you about how to preserve areas around historic buildings for the whole community to enjoy."

When Prince Charles and Lord Mountbatten visited Delhi in February 1975 I was deputed by the government to show them a few sites. Standing on the eastern side of the Red Fort rampart, Lord Mountbatten remarked, "Unless I had seen this—the area that was once stinking slums—I would never have believed the transformation that has been brought about by the development of the River Front."

These are the basic facts. But what is it that is being presented before the Commission? Out of about 600 clearance-cum-resettlement operations organized, only about half a dozen worst cases are being picked up by a "hostile network" headed by R.C. Jain whose personal hostility to me is known to everybody in Delhi. The unanimous agreement of the leading political parties, the cabinet decisions, previous clearances, and past precedents have either been suppressed or underplayed. Side issues and procedural aspects are being magnified—conveniently forgetting that such procedures have been in vogue since the Ministry of Rehabilitation started clearance work in 1963. Shifting of squatters through inducements, incentives, and persuation is the only practical and humane way of dealing with the problem. Had the Delhi Development Authority not provided alternative accommodation, it would not have been possible for various departments of the government and local bodies to acquire lands needed for public purposes, such as schools, roads, and hospitals. Nor could the occupants of these lands make alternative arrangements of shelter on their own. As a matter of fact, the Delhi Development Authority has played a role of humanizing the clearance operations and simultaneously serving the cause of Delhi's development which is mainly in the interest of the poor and have-nots.

It is unfortunate that our experiment got enmeshed in the extraneous factor of high politics of emergency and emotional upsurge during and after the 1977 elections. It is this factor which has blurred the vision of many people, and an essentially humanistic and city planning programme has been made to look inhuman. Is it conceivable that the resettlement colonies, so inhumanly and callously treated as is being made out, would have voted for the erstwhile ruling party when practically every other constituency in the Municipal and Metropolitan Council Election of June 1977 voted against it? I am not concerned with the politics and the elections. My only concern is to demonstrate that the charge of cruel and unjust treatment is totally false.

Allotment of one thousand hectares of developed land in about a year's time to 1.20 lakhs squatter families, on secure tenure, with loan and infrastructural facilities of sufficiently high order, is, in fact, the biggest socialist measure taken in a city of any developing country. Likewise, development of 27 new resettlement colonies with all the components referred to earlier could be legitimately claimed as one of the biggest efforts of our administrative set-up. For comparison, one has to look to Delhi Ajmeri

Gate Scheme (Turkman Gate) which remained pending for over 40 years.

What has been done needs to be judged in the totality of the circumstances and not by isolating one item from the other. The basic test is whether by our efforts, maximum advantage has accrued to the largest number of people in the shortest time, and whether the community and city as a whole have gained both with regard to the current needs and future requirements.

This is the broad topography of my island of truth. The chapters that follow will delineate its other features.

CHAPTER II

THE CONTEXT

> History is no blind goddess and does not excuse blindness in others.
>
> LORD ACTON

Let us first indicate the basic features of the problem of slum and squatter settlements in our metropolitan cities because it is only in the context of the staggering dimensions of the problem and its alarming implications that Delhi's clearance-cum-resettlement operations can be correctly evaluated. A great deal of confusion has been created by those who have neither cared to study the problem in depth, nor work out a feasible alternative approach. In fact, the problem of slums and squatting is one of the least understood problems of our times. One-third of the citizens in developing countries live in miserable shanty-towns, and these are doubling in size every four and half years. "They are not only swelled by population growth, but by the greatest migration in history—a ceaseless tide of people leaving the country."[1] In only two decades, between 1960 and 1980, developing countries like India will have more than doubled its urban population.

If the present trends and attitude persist, migration and squatting would become the gravest problem of the twenty-first century. It will change the very structure of cities in developing countries. It will subvert the pattern of living. It will give rise to new civic and cultural distortions. The squatter settlements will close on a few affluent sectors that may remain in the city, converting them into virtual ghettos. "The city of the developing world faces today one of the most awesome tests in our history."

Squatting is a problem common to all the metropolitan centres in developing countries. "In Africa, squatter settlements constitute 90 per cent of Addis Ababa, 61 per cent of Accra, 33 per cent of Nairobi, and 50 per cent of Menrovia. In Asia, squatter settlements form 29 per cent of Seoul, 31 per cent of Pusan, 67 per cent of Calcutta, 45 per cent of Bombay, 60 per cent of Ankara, and 35 per cent of Manila. In Latin America, squatter settlements form 30 per cent of Ruo de Janeire, 50 per cent of Rocifs, 60 per cent of Begota, 72 per cent of Santo Domingo, 46 per cent of Mexico City, 40 per cent of Lima, and 42 per cent of Caracas."[2] In Tunsia, squatters live in "caves dug out of hill sides." In some South-East Asian cities, there are floating squatter colonies, in junks, boats, and half-sunk ships. Near Mexico City, occupation of public lands by squatters is so rapid that they have earned the name of "squatter parachutists." Existing migration rates, especially in the less developed regions of Africa and Asia, indicate that these percentages will soon increase substantially. In our cities, the squatter population is growing at the rate of about 10 to 12 per cent per annum, which is more than twice the growth rate of these cities.

Defiance of law is implicit in squatting which, literally, means appropriating another's land to one's own use, without right or title. It not only involves slum living in the conventional sense but also forcible occupation of public land. It represents man's acute struggle for shelter in the developing world—a world which has been crippled and maimed by centuries of subjugation and exploitation and which, because of weak economy, absence of administrative dynamism, and lack of enlightened humanism, appears powerless to face the situation.

Squatting shows a wide gap between law and reality. Those who are legal-minded denounce it; those who assume the role of humanist, without any practical obligation to discharge, tend to indulge in polemics and help, perhaps unwittingly, in perpetuation of some of the most inhuman slums in the name of human considerations; while those who know the inner reality and attempt to find a practical solution, consistent with the present and future requirements, have no option but to plunge in a sea of trouble in which they are more likely to be consumed by the high winds of slum politics.

What are the underlying causes of squatting? What are the new forces that are unleashing floods of migrants from rural areas to metropolitan centres of developing countries?

In the West, urbanization was the handmaid of industrialization. The congestion in cities was accompanied by the depopulation of villages. In developing countries like India, the process of urbanization is rather slow, it is disproportionate to the pace of industrialization. It has been correctly described as "rapid urbanization in a context of obdurate underdevelopment." The percentage of urban population greatly exceeds the percentage of working force in industries. A sizable portion of the migrants to cities merely exchange rural for urban misery. Many more people are migrating to cities than their economies can absorb. It has been estimated that between 1950 and 2000, the rural population of developing countries will double to 2.8 billion, while the urban will increase 11 times to 2.2 billion. This increase in urban population will be "more than three times the total urban population of the developed world in 1960." It is estimated that by the turn of the century, 75 per cent of the urban population in the world would be living in cities of developing countries.

The premature and economically unhealthy urbanization, on an extremely fast rate, coupled with the general population explosion, pose a very serious challenge. To meet this challenge in the sphere of shelter and community facilities alone, we need to build "from now onwards to the next twenty years, 10,000 houses, 1,000 schoolrooms and 1,000 hospital wards per day."[3] The challenge also brings us face to face with one of the gravest dilemmas of our times. If we do not encourage substantial migration from villages, these well be swamped with unemployed farmers and labourers. If, on the other hand, we step up migration, our big cities will grow at a disastrous rate and will be overwhelmed by the squatters. In our villages, the land per person has decreased from 1.18 hectares in 1951 to 1.09 hectares in 1971. The number of cultivators has decreased sharply—from 93 million in 1961 to 78 million in 1971—swelling the rank of landless labourers from 27 million to 47 million in the same period.

Already, the conditions are appalling. In India, 44 per cent of the families in urban areas live in one room only. This percentage increases to 67 in the four largest cities, and reaches the fantastic figure of 79 in Calcutta—excluding, of course, thousands who live on the pavements. We have the highest congestion rate in the world—16 to 19 per cent of Indian families live in less than 10 square metres of space.[4]

Even on the basis of the most liberal standards adopted by the

National Building Organization, the current housing shortage in urban India is estimated to be 3.8 million units. Another one million units are needed every year to meet the growing requirements. If the existing backlog has to be cleared in urban areas alone, about Rs 14,000 crores, which is roughly equivalent to 30 per cent of the total investable resources of the current five-year plan, would be needed at an average cost of Rs 16,000 per house. The position is, indeed, desperate. For instance, to house the existing squatters of Calcutta in the conventional low-cost tenements, about hundred years are needed at the current level of investment. This, of course, does not include the growth in squatter population that would take place in the next hundred years.

The position in respect of availability of municipal services is equally depressing. Only 40 per cent of our cities have protected water supply, and that, too, of inferior quality. In July 1971, about 48 per cent of the samples tested in a locality in Bombay turned out to be unfit for human consumption. In respect of sewerage, only 8 per cent of our cities have underground system. Extreme congestion and high densities and use of inferior quality of charcoal and fuel wood by majority of the people to meet their needs of energy cause a high degree of air pollution. Contrary to general impression, concentration of suspended particulate matters, especially carbon monoxide in our cities, is many times more than in the western cities which have acquired notoriety for air pollution due to emissions from automobiles and industries.

The conditions in our villages are no better than in our cities, though the crippling effect on body and soul is somewhat mitigated by the open atmosphere around. Referring to the conditions of Indian villages, Gandhi once said: "Instead of graceful hamlets dotting the land, we have dung heaps. The approach to many villages is not a refreshing experience. Often one would like to shut one's eyes and stuff one's nose; such is the surrounding dirt and offending smell." The conditions have not materially changed since then, and the dirt and offending smell still greet us in most of the villages.

A few typical studies conducted earlier in villages revealed that the problems of congestion, sanitation, and water supply were as acute in rural India as in the worst slums of metropolitan areas. While in rural areas, the percentage of houses owned was greater than in urban areas, the floor space per capita was only

58 sq. ft. The number of rooms per tenement was less; sanitation and ventilation were worse; and farm produce, fodder, and cattle competed with men for space in residential houses. Only 19 per cent of our rural houses are pucca and only about 3.4 per cent are well ventilated and fulfil the norms of healthy living.

Paucity of resources and low levels of income are major handicaps. A recent World Bank study of five typical cities of developing countries—Madras, Ahemdabad, Nairobi, Mexico City, and Bogota—reveals that it is only the richest 30 to 50 per cent of the urban population who can afford to live in the cheapest tenements built by public authorities. And this calculation is based upon the optimistic assumption that poor people can afford to earmark 15 per cent of their income for housing. Actually, 75 per cent of income of such people is spent on food and 19 to 23 per cent on other basic necessities like clothing and medical care. Only 6 to 10 per cent is left for housing. Thus, even a smaller percentage than what has been worked out by the World Bank can afford to buy the cheapest tenement for low-income groups. Recent surveys of public housing projects in northern India also indicate that out of every ten houses being built for the poor, seven to nine are actually used by the better class of people.

Another impediment is our somewhat indifferent and superficial society. Those who are in a better position are not alive to their responsibilities towards the weaker sections. They would like to have their clothes washed from *dhobies*, get their shoes polished and repaired from cobblers, and have their houses cleaned from sweepers, but they would not like to contribute anything in the shape of land or structures for them. Added to this are the problems inherent in our social and economic imbalances which no city planning can solve. The structural legacy of our old cities creates its own problem.

It is because of these underlying causes that squatter population has been rapidly increasing in metropolitan cities like Delhi, Bombay, and Calcutta. A large number of people come daily from the impoverished rural areas and occupy every available vacant space for setting up shacks of wood, tin or card-board thereon. No site is too slushy, too filthy, and too dangerous for a precarious huddle of huts to be put up and for human beings to dwell in them. In their tattered misery, squatters mock the aspirations of all those who yearn to make their cities sophisticated and modern. They serve as visible reminders of the economic and social injustices that still plague our society.

In 1973 in Delhi, there was one squatter household for every five non-squatter households, whereas in 1951, there was one squatter household for every twenty non-squatter households. In absolute number, there were 12,746 squatter families in 1951, 22,415 in 1956, 42,814 in 1961, 77,693 in 1966, 1,15,961 in 1971, and 1,41,757 in 1973.[5]

In the circumstances, will haphazard and disorganized squatting, with consequent wastage of resources, help any one? Will the general environmental degradation be in the interest of squatters' health and happiness? Will it be wise to close our eyes to the gathering storm and not evolve a long-term policy to meet the challenge of new forces sweeping the developing world? Will it not be worthwhile to concentrate efforts on innovative techniques which can convert our liabilities into assets?

The growing pressure of population and absence of corresponding development leave hardly any choice between the rural and urban misery. The migrant is squezeed out of the village because of worsening poverty and mounting pressure on land, while the city is not in a position to absorb him and provide any shelter worth the name. He is literally caught between the two worlds—"one dead, the other not yet born." But the process of migration is difficult to reverse or contain. The migrant has to fight it out in the city. A popular song of the urban squatter in Brazil expresses the spirit:

I may be arrested, I may be hit,
I may not even have something to eat.
But I won't change my opinion.
I won't ever move from this hill.

If there is no water I'll dig myself a well.
If there is no meat, I'll buy a bone.
And put it in the soup—I'll get on, I'll get on.

This spirit has to be made use of. It is an asset, not a liability. The cities have got to be prepared to absorb the migrants. More planned and purposive the process of absorption, the better it would be for the migrant and the city.

We should understand our limited options. We must recognize that we have problem not of housing in the conventional sense, but of "shelter"; not of comfortable or luxurious living, but of "roof over the head"; not of having spacious colonies, but of avoiding extreme congestion and creating an atmosphere in which personality is not stifled.

The reality warns us. The context is merciless. The avalanche cannot be simply wished away. If we are willing to explore new avenues, if we have the vision to discard obsolete notions, if we have the courage to stand up to vested interests and not allow inhuman slums in the name of human considerations, we may be able to save the situation and even solve the problem. If, on the other hand, we continue to drag our feet and play to the gallery, and hope for something to turn up, nothing but disaster awaits our cities and we would have none but ourselves to blame. History is no blind goddess and does not excuse blindness in others. It would maim and crush us under its heels.

CHAPTER III

BACKGROUND AND THE PRE-EMERGENCY DAYS

> The philosopher asks, what is truth? He does not ask what is currently accepted? He asks what is true for every body? Truth does not know the frontiers of political geography.
>
> KARL MARX

To meet the challenge of rapid urbanization and to prevent haphazard development, Jawaharlal Nehru conceived the idea of setting up a single planning authority for the entire metropolitan region. Accordingly, the Delhi Development Act was formulated and passed by Parliament in 1957, and the Delhi Development Authority undertook the task of formulation of a Master Plan under the statutory provisions of the Act. After publication of the draft Master Plan and inviting public objections, the Delhi Development Authority prepared the final Master Plan and it was enforced with effect from 1 September 1962. It had the approval of the Union Cabinet and Parliament. The Master Plan (1962-1981) assessed the existing deficiencies in various directions—housing, community facilities, water, power, transport, etc.—and estimated future requirements. To hold the projected population of 46 lakhs, the Plan envisaged urbanization of about 1,10,000 acres of land up to 1981 as against 42,600 acres in 1960. It stipulated that 42 per cent of the area should be earmarked for residential use, 23.7 per cent for recreational and green use, 8 per cent for public utilities, 7.4 per cent for government offices, 5.4 per cent for industrial use, 2.3 per cent for commercial use and the remaining land for circulation, institutional use, and other community facilities. In other words, a rational synthesis of various needs of the community was attempted to bring about balanced development of the city. Obviously, the areas needed for public utilities, community facilities, such as roads, bridges, schools, hospitals and the like, could not be allowed to be squatted upon.

THE SCHEME AND ITS BRIEF HISTORY

In 1960, when preparation of the Delhi Master Plan was in hand, a scheme, known as Squatter Resettlement Scheme, was formulated to deal with the problem of slums and squatting on public lands. It was sanctioned by the Union Cabinet in 1960. The scheme envisaged removal of squatters from public lands and allotment of alternative plots to them in colonies to be developed for the purpose. A special census of squatters was conducted in June-July 1960, and only those squatters who were enumerated in this census were declared eligible for alternative accommodation. Persons occupying public lands after the census (July 1960) were to be treated as "ineligible" and they were to be evicted without provision of any alternative accommodation. The scheme, I must make it clear, did not take into consideration the factors brought out by me in the preceding chapter. At the time of its formulation, there was hardly any recognition of the fact that new forces of unprecedented magnitude and complexity were sweeping the city. Nevertheless, the scheme was somewhat of an innovation. It recognized the need for alternative accommodation and also for the planned development and environmental upgradation of the city.

The salient features of the scheme, as originally envisaged, were allotment of 80 sq. yds. of plots to each eligible squatter family on a 99-year lease basis. The plot was to be provided with a latrine, a water tap, and a plinth on which the allottee could build a hut or a house according to his need. The scheme was entrusted to the Delhi Municipal Corporation for implementation.

During the course of implementation, a number of practical difficulties arose. It was noticed that the provisions of the scheme were misused with impunity. The allottees soon sold their plots on monetary considerations to comparatively well-to-do persons and again squatted elsewhere on public land. It was also noticed that, majority of the squatters were unable to pay the monthly instalment of Rs 12.79. Accordingly, the scheme was revised with the approval of the Union Cabinet. The revised scheme eliminated the element of ownership and provided for allotment of open developed plots or small tenements on rents. It was thought that, out of the 50,000 eligible squatters, not more than 5,000 would be in a position to take a tenement on rent and not more than 20,000 would be able to afford the rent of open developed plots of 80 sq. yds. Accordingly, provision was made for construction of 5,000 tenements and development of 20,000 plots. For the remaining 25,000 families who could afford only low rent, it was decided to allot 25 sq. yds. plots on a monthly rent of Rs 3-50 plus water and conservancy charges of Re 1 per month. Those plots were to be provided common facilities for water and sanitation as well as street lighting.

During the course of implementation of the revised scheme, it was found that "eligible" and "ineligible" squatters were intermixed. As it was difficult to clear areas without removing both "eligible" and "ineligible" squatters, it was decided by the government in May 1964 to allot camping sites of 25 sq. yds. each, even to "ineligible" squatters in far off colonies on payment of full rent as compared to subsidized rent charged from "eligibles" squatters.

The Scheme and Political Parties

As the problem proved much more complex than was originally thought, a comprehensive review of the scheme was undertaken in 1967. A high level Study Group was appointed by the Home Minister under the chairmanship of the Minister for Works and Housing, Jagan Nath Rao. Besides the Chairman, the members of the Study Group were Dr A.N. Jha, Lieutenant Governor, Vijay Kumar Malhotra, Chief Executive Councillor, Hans Raj, Mayor, Kidar Nath Sahni, Chairman of the Standing Committee of Delhi Municipal Corporation, Shiv Charan Gupta, leader of the opposition in the Metropolitan Council, Des Raj Choudhry, leader of the opposition in the Delhi Municipal Corporation, Kanwar Lal Gupta, MP, Brahm Parkash, MP, Santokh Singh, MP, and Miss Surinder Saini, Senior Vice-President of New Delhi Municipal Committee.

During the deliberations of the Study Group, one of the basic points that clearly emerged was that the problem of squatting would be incapable of solution if politics got injected in it. At the very outset, therefore, the Study Group unanimously agreed that the squatter problem in Delhi would be treated entirely as "non-political both inside the Group as well as outside."

The Study Group estimated that in August 1967, there were about 66,000 "post-July 1960" squatters and 34,000 "pre-July 1960" squatters. The former category was termed as "ineligible" and the latter as "eligible." Keeping in view the financial constraints and the paucity of land and the desirability of liquidating the problem expeditiously, the Study Group recommended that further construction of tenements and development of plots of 80 sq. yds. should be abandoned and in lieu thereof larger number of plots of 25 sq. yds. should be developed for resettlement of squatters. It also recommended that 66,000 "ineligible" squatter families should be removed to the periphery of the city where minimum facilities like drinking water and community latrines should be provided.

The above unanimous recommendations of the Study Group were accepted by the central government and modifications made in the scheme accordingly. Incensed by the problem of squatting the Study Group had also recommended that squatting on public land should be made a cognizable offence punishable for imprisonment up to three years. This recommendation, too, was accepted by the government in principle, and further action was to be taken to give it a legal shape.

What do the above stipulations of the scheme and thinking of the government and the Study Group comprising representatives of leading political parties on the subject show? These stipulations clearly indicate that all of them were keen to deal with the problem firmly and shift the squatters to the periphery of the city where they wanted minimum facilities of drinking water and community latrines to be provided. Further, they wanted to make squatting on public land a cognizable offence. Therefore, the Delhi Development Authority had to act broadly within the framework of the above scheme which, incidentally, is even operative today. In view of the above facts, is it fair to blame the Delhi Development Authority?

In fact, what was done by the Delhi Development Authority during the emergency is more liberal, more just and humane than what was envisaged in the scheme sanctioned by the Government of India on the basis of the recommendations of the Study Group. For instance, although the government orders envisaged resettlement of squatters in the periphery of the city, yet majority of the 27 resettlement colonies were developed within the urbanizable limits on some of the most costly lands available at that time. Take, for instance, the resettlement colony of Shakurpur. Here, about 10,000 families, comprising a population of about 50,000, have been resettled. The colony is located right on the Ring Road, opposite one of the most thriving industrial colony of Lawrence Road. In Delhi Development Authority's residential colony of Paschimpuri, which is about two to three miles away from the city than the resettlement colony of Shakurpur, residential plots have been selling at the rate of about Rs 300 per sq. yd. Likewise, the Mangolpuri resettlement site is opposite the Paschimpuri residential colony. It has a population of about one lakh, and covers valuable lands. If market value of these lands are calculated, the extent of the benefit given to the resettlers, who have an option to keep the plot on nominal rent or purchase it on nominal price or hire-purchase basis, would become self-evident.

Again, for most of the squatters the government scheme envisaged "provision of absolutely minimum facilities like drinking water and community latrines, particularly for women." Against this stipulation, the Delhi Development Authority provided even for the ineligible squatters, which constituted majority of the squatter population, fully developed plots, metalled roads, brick paved pathways, tubewells, public hydrants, storm water drain, culverts, street lighting, parks and playgrounds, water borne community latrines, schools, dispensaries, post offices, milk booth, television-cum-community centres, etc. Moreover, it is not only the scale of amenities but the speed with which these were made available that was significant. Previously, it took a long time to provide such facilities.

Before we go into the details of what was done with regard to removal and resettlement of squatters during the emergency, it is necessary to refer to what happened in the period before the emergency and what was the thinking of the government and public men on the subject. It will be better to deal with this period in two parts: (*i*) the period from 1967-68 to January 1972 and (*ii*) January 1972 to June 1975.

Dr A.N. Jha's Time

The Squatter Resettlement Scheme was sanctioned by the Government of India in 1960 and its implementation was entrusted to the Delhi Municipal Corporation. The central government was, however, not satisfied with the performance of the Delhi Municipal Corporation. It, therefore, decided in 1967-68 to entrust the implementation of the scheme to the Delhi Development Authority.

A vigorous clearance-cum-resettlement-cum-redevelopment drive was launched by the DDA in 1967-68. The first major operation was undertaken in the Yamuna Bazar area near Nigam Bodh Ghat, between the Yamuna and the city wall. The Ghat is a sacred and historical site. Its antiquity dates back to Pandava's time. Yudisthra is believed to have performed Asvamadha Yagya here around 1500 B.C., when Inderprastha, the present site of Purana Quilla, was the capital of Pandava Kingdom.

Notwithstanding the historical antiquity, sacred character of the Nigam Bodh Ghat, the natural beauty of the River Front and its green land use, the site had been allowed to become a vast stinking slum with about 6,000 squatters, scores of cattle dairies, and about 700 non-conforming industries and godowns. The land was slushy, uneven, and floodable with hardly any drainage, latrines and clean water supply. It was the foulest nauseating slum, incapable of being developed or serviced at reasonable cost. Yet vested interests, political as well as financial, prevented the clearance of this slum and relocation of about 30,000 people in healthier environment with proper layouts and basic civic amenities. All this was done in the name of human considerations. Politics could not trade in human misery in worse form.

The damage done to the general environment and the cityscape was equally distressing. Once, in the late fifties, Dr Rajendra Prasad, former President of India, went to Nigam Bodh Ghat in connection with the creamation ceremony of one of his relations. Some members of the diplomatic corps also attended the ceremony. Apart from the fact that he himself was deeply moved by what he saw, his national pride was hurt by the reaction of some diplomats who could hardly stand the stench, filth, and flies all around. On return, with poetic pain and anguish, he wrote a letter to the Chief Commissioner. He suggested that immediate steps should be taken to remove the slummy conditions, improve the environment, and restore the sanctity of Nigam Bodh Ghat. Yet, such was the stranglehold of the politics of slums, nothing was done for years. The area remained a spectacle of national shame and human misery in its worst form. Earlier, Jawaharlal Nehru had unsuccessfully intervened to get a portion of the slum cleared for completion of the Ring Road near the Monkey Bridge.

It was the determination and courage of Dr A.N. Jha, Chief Commissioner and later Lieutenant Governor of Delhi, which resulted in the clearance of the abominable slum of Yamuna Bazar. One day, after visiting the site with me, he asked: "Can we clear this"? "Yes, certainly," I replied, "provided political element can be taken care of." Dr Jha took little time to decide. He said, "We must go ahead. Be careful. In the process, we may lose our jobs, even our heads."

I believe that Dr Jha was impelled to take the quick decision because of his strong orientation towards development and his deep regard for our history and cultural heritage. He was, however, doubtful about the administrative feasibility of implementing this project in two or three days. He knew that if it took longer, vested interests would intervene with full force and the clearance operation would have to be abandoned half-way.

I spoke to the squatters direct. I explained to them the long-term advantages of moving to Seelampur and Seemapuri, where resettlement colonies had been planned and developed with basic civic facilities. Some responded favourably, some were sceptical, and some, particularly those who are popularly called *dadas*, were hostile. I avoided the political element to the extent I could.

I drew up a plan of action, and explained it to Dr Jha. I was surprised to note that, though he was keen to secure help for me from other departments of the Delhi administration, he was not interested in knowing the framework of my programme. He reposed full confidence in me. After discussions with him, I was left with no doubt that if I succeeded I would be applauded and given full credit, and if I failed, I would be sympathized with and protected. Such was the attitude of our great civil servants like Dr A.N. Jha, Bhagwan Sahya, Dharma Vira, and Vishwanathan. Contrast it with those who nowadays let their officers be treated like masterless dogs, and are also willing to add a whip or two on their own.

The D-day arrived. On 17 June 1967 the clearance operation began. Every item of work was executed with precision. About 300 trucks were pressed into service. In about three days, the clearance work and simultaneous resettlement was completed.

Immediately after the shifting, bulldozers were pressed into service. The area was levelled, and the work of developing the River Front and laying down of a garden taken in hand. Horticulturists, engineers, planners, and administrators worked round the clock to translate a dream into reality. A new missionary zeal had gripped the entire set-up. It almost became a regular feature with Dr Jha to invite me to his residential office, drive to the site, discuss the progress with the field officers, encourage them, and regale all of us with his anecdotes and humorous tales. Dr Jha took Vijay Kumar Malhotra, Chief Executive Councillor, Hans Raj Gupta, Mayor, K.N. Sahni, Chairman of the Standing Committee, in confidence, and respected their suggestions.

The River Front project was never conceived in a formal, hardbound framework. It grew informally, almost collectively, from the minds of all those involved. Seeing the area today, in its simplicity and charm against its historical and cultural legacy, it appears to have sprung from the soil as truly as folk music springs from the soul of the people. The relief sculpture on the entrance wall of the Nigam Bodh Ghat represents the cycle of life, reminds us of our great philosophy and thought, of the transitory nature of our existence, and of our duty in this universe and our mission beyond.

The radical change that took place in the environment of the Nigam Bodh Ghat, Yamuna Bazar, and the River Front pleased the lovers of the city. In connection with a land dispute of Yamuna Bazar, a case came before the High Court against the Delhi Development Authority. The lawyer of the opposite party started a harangue against the Authority. The presiding officer of the court remarked: "The Delhi Development Authority has done a wonderful job in the area. Now, I will not be even unhappy to die because my soul will pass through that beautiful garden and delightful environment." Such was the reaction of the right-thinking people. Unfortunately, in our country, knowledgeable persons seldom speak in public. They usually confine their talk to their drawing rooms, while vested interests continue to indulge in propaganda and create wrong impressions in the public mind.

On 19 January 1972, Dr Jha, unfortunately, passed away after a brief illness. According to the family custom, he was cremated not at the Nigam Bodh Ghat but at a site little away on the bank of the river. As a token of his contribution to the city's development, a small smadhi type memorial was proposed to be constructed at the site of cremation. A special meeting of the Executive Council was held on 19 January 1972 under the chairmanship of Lieutenant Governor, M.G. Pimputkar. The Council resolved that a suitable memorial should be built in memory of Dr A.N. Jha. Unfortunately, this was never implemented. The bureaucratic jealousies scuttled the proposal. The administration had begun to move in narrow grooves.

It is sad that this ungrateful city did not even build a small memorial to Dr Jha. He achieved a great deal, and that was not without trouble. At the time of Yamuna Bazar clearance, 18-20 June 1967, 107 persons, including Santokh Singh, MP, and Shiv Charan Gupta, leader of the Congress Party in the Metropolitan Council, were arrested for defying Section 144 Cr. PC which had been earlier promulgated in the area.[1]

The two main political parties, the Congress and the Jan Sangh, started blaming each other. Kishore Lal issued a statement on behalf of the Delhi Pradesh Congress on 20 June 1967. He said, "Yamuna Bazar was a Congress stronghold and the administration's action was aimed at embarrassing the Congress Party and its supporters." On the same day, Vijay Kumar Malhotra, Chief Executive Councillor, commented, "The local Congress leaders are shedding crocodile tears. Instead of resorting to the so-called satyagraha, the Pradesh Congress leaders should have approached the ministry in the central government for revision of the scheme under which encroachments on public lands were being removed and slums cleared." He also reminded the Congress leaders that in the meeting of the ad-hoc Slum Clearance Committee, held on 22 January 1964, which was attended by the then Works and Housing Minister, Mehar Chand Khanna, it was decided to clear all the squatted areas of the city.[2] On 22 June 1967, in the Lok Sabha when Bibhuti Mishra, Congress MP, criticized Jan Sangh administration, Kanwar Lal Gupta and Hardayal Devgun, Jan Sangh members of Parliament, accused the Congressmen of picking up a row, not because shacks were cleared from Yamuna Bazar, but because the unauthorized godown of the erstwhile Congress Mayor was removed by the Delhi Development Authority. The politics and slum clearance were getting more and more enmeshed.

Exasperated by the attitudes exhibited in public, Dr Jha told the Home Minister, Y.B. Chavan, in March 1968:

> To me the attitude of ambivalence on the part of the political parties has been to say the least most disappointing. On the one hand, they all agreed unanimously that ineligible squatters be removed and no additional funds be provided, and at the same time they criticize the central government and myself for not providing all the amenities. I must, in the end, confess to a feeling of having been personally let down by every one and shown up as one who has been acting arbitrarily and tyrannically—the only person lacking in sympathy while every one else has been falling over each other to be human and helpful and generous.

Some elements were bent upon exploiting the issue politically. On 27 July 1967, they staged a noisy demonstration and burnt the effigy of Dr Jha, "complete with goggles, and a pipe, after beating it with lathies and shoes." But Dr Jha's equanimity and sense of humour never deserted him. When, after a few days of the demonstration, Mir Mushtaq Ahmed rang up to ask for appointment, Dr Jha replied: "Mir Sahib, you have to come to heaven because your friends have already sent me there."[3]

The knowledgeable section of the press, however, supported the drive. In its editorial of 24 June 1967, the *Hindustan Times* commented:

> Today the Jhuggi-Jhonpri problem is not one of housing and homeless. Indulgence towards them has not only provided a shield for the unscrupulous land speculators but has also

enabled commercial concerns to take advantage of the authorities' lack of concern about land rights. It is doubtful if prominent Congressmen would have offered to go to jail if the displaced jhuggi-dwellers' comfort was the only question involved. Congress have all along been a party to the decision for removal of slums. But perhaps they never realized that their successors in office would start with Yamuna Bazar and begin to remind everyone that the demolition is in accordance with a Central Government decision....

The homeless in Delhi, whose number is progressively increasing, deserve every consideration, but if they are a pawn in the hands of middlemen and the unscrupulous among the officials and politicians, it is time they were segregated. They must no longer be exploited by politicians, junior officials and others who benefit because of their helplessness.

I have considered it necessary to deal with Yamuna Bazar clearance and River Front developments in some details, because it explains every material aspect of the problem, particularly the emerging attitude of ambivalence.

Subsequently, other ugly spots were taken up for clearance and development. The area around Hanuman Temple had acquired notoriety for its insanitary conditions. The temple was built by Maharaja Jai Singh (1699-1743)—Delhi's residents are particularly devoted to it. Behind the smoke screen of religion, the Mahant derived considerable pecuniary benefits from unauthorized shops, coal depots, motor repair workshops, and shacks. When the clearance work in the area was taken up on 22 July 1967, about 2,000 empty beer bottles were recovered from a smelly stall stuck to the rear wall of the temple. Yet attempts were made by the Mahant to whip up public agitation on the ground of desecration of religious places.

Idgah, near Jat Ki Phari, is another such religious and historical site. From the religious angle, this mosque is even more important than Jama Masjid. The Mughal emperor, Aurangzeb, and President Fakhruddin Ali Ahmed used to offer their Id prayers in Idgah. The surroundings of the mosque were marred by a vast, sprawling slum, comprising godowns, kabari-stores, workshops, etc. The mosque was hardly visible. A few self-styled "Mutawalis," who were not recognized by the Wakf Board, claimed the public land around the mosque as religious and collected huge sum and pocketed it themselves. When the clearance was done, they made every effort to exploit the religious sentiments and accused the officials of grabbing the land and damaging the mosque, although the Delhi Development Authority merely developed a beautiful garden which enhanced the architectural simplicity of the monument, upgraded its environment, and provided the much needed "patch of green" to the suffocating population of Qasabpura and Motia Khan.

The clearance of Parsad Nagar slum on 17-19 November 1968, where now Rajindra Place stands, had its own turmoil. Allegations similar to those which are now being made in respect of the Turkman Gate clearance were levelled by certain political elements. In Parliament Questions Nos. 534-537, put up in January 1969, reference was made to forcible demolition of about 10,000 houses in Parsad Nagar and Amritkaur Puri and bulldozing of some of the locked premises. A death under the bulldozer was also alleged. Such false allegations and exaggerated versions of minor incidents are part of a technique to browbeat the authorities, and this technique has not changed over a period of time.

Similar clearance-cum-development operations were taken in many other areas—Patel Nagar Hillock, Kela Godown, Gurdwara Moti Bagh, Kotla Ferozeshah, Tilak Bridge, Ghata Masjid, Phool Walon-Ki-Sair, etc.

After the initial storm, however, everything settled down. The squatters realized the long-term benefits which accrued to them. The cityscape improved and even the critics as well as those who disowned responsibility for clearance started describing Delhi as the "city of smiles." Even the Public Accounts Committee of Parliament, which is usually critical of the government performance, remarked, "there has been improvement after the transfer of the Scheme to the Delhi Development Authority."[4]

The drive also exposed commercial interests in squatting which operated in a subtle way behind the scene. In this regard, it is interesting to recall a report of *Patriot* (16 September 1967) which read: "The demolition squad that brought down unauthorised structures in Darya Ganj yesterday has unearthed a queer set-up—a millionaire owned one of the unauthorised structures. This he had leased out as workshop. He has now lined up with the others for alternative accommodation." In another case of clearance on 30 June 1967, 30 truck load of tents had to be lifted from the tomb of the famous Sufi saint, Shah Wali Ulhah Mahaddis, on Mirdard Road, inside the complex of Lok Nayak Jayaparkash Narain Hospital and Maulana Azad College.[5]

The Wakf or Sunni Majlis-e-Aukaf land and the public area around religious and historical monuments have been special hunting grounds of commercial interests. For instance, on the site around Durgaha Nizamuddin, including the lands in immediate vicinity of the grave of Mirza Ghalib, the famous Urdu poet, scores of petty workshops, godowns, shacks, and cattle dairies had been set up by powerful commercial interests who were collecting large "rents" illegally. When all these establishments were cleared in 1969, vested interests tried to mislead Fakhruddin Ali Ahmed who was Minister for Wakf at that time and even succeeded temporarily, by misrepresenting that old graves, including the grave of Sheikh Abdullah's mother, had been "bulldozed" by the Delhi Development Authority, although the fact was that before the clearance, motor workshops and cattle dairies were located right on the graves and had caused considerable damage to them. The DDA fenced, cleaned, and grassed the area around the graves and other old monuments, thus saving them from extinction. A beautiful lawn and row of little trees and shrubs have now emerged all along the link road from Sunder Nagar to Jangpura.

All the cleared areas were redeveloped and studded with large varieties of trees and flowers. Instead of disgraceful slums, which marred the face of our ancient and historic metropolis, we have beautiful parks and gardens, freshness and fragrance from which would act as a tonic to the citizens of Delhi for generations to come.

Resettlement of squatters at proper site, with secure tenure, was also in the interest of the squatters. Today, all of them are happy and find themselves amidst thriving colonies. In fact, there is persistent demand from various quarters to get accommodation in these colonies.

ELECTIONS

Unfortunately, it were the pressure groups and vested interests which confused the public for their own selfish ends. They deliberately suppressed the positive aspects of the clearance-cum-resettlement-cum-redevelopment programme and blew out of all proportion the temporary hardship inherent in such a programme. Sponsored news story were published, and if any one tried to explain the correct position, he was dubbed as an inhuman devil.

Election time was particularly exploited by pressure groups and vested interests. The politics of slums was perfected. Behind the smoke screen of "human consideration" a strong base for political and financial power was created. The commercial squatters, such as builders of shops and stalls around cinemas, were a class by themselves. They derived considerable pecuniary advantage and were always willing to buy protection of the powerful interest by making available "voluntary agitators and demonstrators."

Pressure groups and vested interests played their game in such a subtle way that the government had no other option but to succumb to their pressure. The vicious circle made it inevitable that all major political parties championed the cause of squatters and illegal encroachers and builders. Those who did not favour their cause were dubbed as unsympathetic to the the poor. The moral degradation came to such a pass that those who violated law benefitted immeasurably, particularly from commercial squatting and illegal sales of land, while those who respected law suffered. Any officer who took a firm stand was soon "demolished" by subtle means, such as making use of a section of labour unions or some disgruntled elements in the office. False complaints were got engineered. Honest and straightforward decisions to secure expeditious disposal were twisted. The officer was hounded till he slowed down. If one has to see the moral crisis through which our society was, and is still passing, one has to study in depth the "politics of slums, squatting, unauthorized construction and illegal sales" in Delhi.

JANUARY 1972-JUNE 1975

The climate, which dominated the period January 1972 to

June 1975, existed earlier. But it gained ascendancy during January 1972 to June 1975. With the passing of Dr Jha, in fact, ended a phase of Delhi's development. Thereafter, petty jealousies and intrigues took firm grip, and service to the cause of Delhi's development became a liability—a constant source of trouble and harassment.

The Study Group referred to earlier had unanimously resolved that the issue of squatters and slums would be treated as non-political. But this resolution was followed more in breach than in honour. Nevertheless, the central government continued to express from time to time its concern over increasing menace of unauthorized construction, encroachments, and illegal sales. This would be evident from various meetings and pronouncements. In early 1972, a high-level meeting was held under the chairmanship of Uma Shankar Dixit, Union Minister for Works and Housing. In the meeting, it was agreed that unauthorized constructions, which came in the way of construction of bridges and road alignments, should be taken up for clearance in the first instance. Unauthorized structures on lands which were earmarked for hospitals, schools, and colleges should be taken up for clearance in the second stage; and in the third stage all other unauthorized constructions should be cleared as soon as possible to provide alternative accommodation to the concerned persons. A meeting was also held under the chairmanship of the Lieutenant Governor on 18 April 1972 in which it was decided that the demolition squad of the Delhi Development Authority could be pressed in service, wherever needed, by any agency and there was no use wasting resources on duplicating such arrangements. If there was apprehension of breach of law and order, the police help should be promptly made available. Another high-level meeting was held on 21 May 1973 under the chairmanship of Bhola Paswan Shastri, Union Minister for Works and Housing. The meeting was attended by senior officers of the various ministries/departments. The need to take firm action against unauthorized encroachments and squatting was emphasized by the participants. It was felt that effective action was possible if lands under the management of various ministries/departments were transferred to the Delhi Development Authority as it was the only agency which could deal effectively with the problem and develop the sites once they were cleared. Prime Minister Indira Gandhi herself was alarmed over the increasing menace of unauthorized encroachments and illegal constructions. In July 1974, she herself called two meetings and impressed upon the ministries, departments and organizations concerned to deal with the problem firmly and remove legal and administrative bottlenecks.

DIR OR MISA

It was not only the government but also various non-officials who were asking for drastic remedies, such as use of Defence of India Rule and Maintenance of Internal Security Act for dealing with the unauthorized encroachments and construction. As reported in the *Hindustan Times* (20 August 1974), two public men urged the use of Defence of India Rule. The relevant report is reproduced below:

> Mr. Kishori Lal, Leader of the Congress Party in the Municipal Corporation, today demanded that the Defence of India Rule be invoked against the colonisers in order to check the growth of unauthorised colonies in the capital.

A similar report also appeared in the *Times of India* (20 August 1974). It read:

> Mr. Kishori Lal, Leader of the Congress Party in the Delhi Municipal Corporation, today urged the Union Home Minister to invoke the provisions of the Defence of India Rule or Maintenance of Internal Security Act to book unscrupulous colonisers who were duping innocent citizens in land deals. In a letter to Mr. Uma Shankar Dikshit, Mr. Kishori Lal had referred to the law and order review meeting presided over by the Lt. Governor on July 11.
>
> At the meeting, Mr. Vijay Kumar Malhotra, President of the Delhi Pradesh Jan Sangh, had raised the issue of large-scale encroachment on public land and emergence of unauthorised colonies on land earmarked for green areas. Mr. K.N. Sahani, Mayor, had pointed out that police pro-

tection was not available to Delhi Municipal Corporation demolition staff and this made removal of such encroachment difficult.

Mr. Kishori Lal asked the Jan Sangh leaders to discuss the use of Defence of India Rule and Maintenance of Internal Security Act at the Party level to curb such encroachment and decide to support this move in the interest of planned development in the Capital.

In spite of various meetings and pronouncements, the clearance-cum-resettlement operations remained in comparatively low key during this period. The main reasons for this were:

(a) Apart from the political factors referred above, the government departments took time to transfer the lands to the Delhi Development Authority. Thus, the multiple control over public lands remained. This was a serious handicap in taking effective action. The Lieutenant Governor made it clear time and again that he would take action only after the lands were transferred to the Delhi Development Authority.

(b) A point had been raised by I.K. Gujral, Minister of State for Works and Housing, about the cost of removal of squatters. In 1973-74, instructions were issued by the government that cost of removal should be met by the departments which owned the land. Considerable correspondence and delay occurred because of this issue and clearance-cum-resettlement work was held up.

(c) Immediately after the appointment of R.C. Jain as Special Assistant to Baleshwar Prasad, Lieutenant Governor, Jain's batchmate, R. Shankaran, was appointed as Commissioner in the Delhi Development Authority. Jain started dealing directly with Shankaran, a subordinate of the Vice-Chairman, thus violating the established administrative norms and conventions. I was totally cut off. Naturally, in such a set-up the work of clearance and development suffered badly, particularly because Shankaran had neither any knowledge of local conditions nor any experience of urban development work.

(d) The instructions issued in 1972 by Baleshwar Prasad

Background and the Pre-Emergency Days 43

were that SDM, police and the landowning departments should check unauthorized encroachments. The area of responsibility was, therefore, somewhat diffused. On the other hand, during the emergency or shortly before it, all the major landowning departments handed over their lands to the Delhi Development Authority.

(e) Due to preoccupation of the police with the labour agitation and other law and order problems, the police help was not always available to deal with vested interests. In this connection, the complaint of the then Mayor, Kedar Nath Sahni, about the non-availability of the police to the Corporation is relevant.

From the above, however, it should not be inferred that no clearance operations were carried out during January 1272 to June 1975. The clearance-cum-resettlement operations undoubtedly increased during the emergency, but such operations were undertaken on a large scale earlier also. In 1974, for instance, about 150 clearance operations were organized. The number of squatters involved may be comparatively small, but the number of operations was not insignificant. Comparatively large clearances included clearance of Rampur, Shahjada Bagh, Sheikh Sarai, Chiragh Delhi, Seelampur, Jhandewalan, Najafgarh Road, Dr Krishna Road, Tihar, INA area, Pandav Nagar, etc.

Excellent results were achieved in certain areas, particularly in regard to the clearance of lands around Purana Quilla, Mazar "Tusi" and lands earmarked for National Botanical Garden in the Mehrauli complex. Of course, agitations were organized by vested interests for a number of days. But can any one who knows the conditions prevailing in these areas before the clearance and the conditions now existing doubt that the trouble was worth facing? During January 1972 to January 1975, political factors did constitute a constraint, but much better results could have been achieved if the administration had shown the same courage, the same dynamism, the same regard for city's cultural heritage, and the same sense of timing and coordination as was exhibited during Dr A.N. Jha's time. Personality and organization are always inter-related, but in a developing country like India, beset as it is with routine and timid notions of administration, the impact a powerful personality can make a world of difference on the organization.

CHAPTER IV

THE EMERGENCY DAYS

> The time is out of joint—O cursed Spite, that ever I was born to set it right
>
> HAMLET

During the emergency, the same scheme, the same policy, and the same procedures were continued; only the pace of work increased. The government had always intended to remove the squatters and liquidate the problem in the shortest possible time. The original time-limit fixed for completion of the resettlement work was only two years. The Public Accounts Committee of Parliament had also exhorted the government to "speedily implement the scheme as already sanctioned." Even the work of slum clearance under the Slum Areas (Improvement and Clearance) Act, 1956, which was earlier entrusted to Delhi Municipal Corporation, was transferred by the central government to the Delhi Development Authority in February 1974, with a view to "securing expeditious and efficient implementation" of the old pending schemes in respect of which Corporation's performance had not been satisfactory.

All that happened after the declaration of the emergency was that the government resolved to be firm and put in sustained efforts to implement what it had always intended to implement. Negative factors set out earlier no longer existed. The mood of the slum-dwellers was also in favour of shifting, and to take advantage of the incentives and inducement provided.

In connection with the Cultural Award given to me by the Australian Government in May 1975, I left for Sydney a day after the declaration of the emergency. It appears that during my absence a decision had been taken to shift the slum and squatter settlements and non-conforming trades and accord priority to this work. In pursuance of this decision, a major clearance operation of Old Subzimandi was undertaken under the orders and supervision of Lieutenant Governor Kishan Chand. On my return from Australia in mid-July 1975, I was informed by him about this operation and of the government's resolve to speed up the clearance of slum and squatter settlements.

Shortly afterwards, in August 1975, a meeting on the subject was held under the chairmanship of the Prime Minister at her residential office. This meeting was called at the request of the local members of Parliament. It was organized by the Home Ministry, and was attended, among others, by the Minister of State in the Home Ministry, all local members of Parliament, Chief Executive Councillor, and prominent non-officials like Chairman of the Metropolitan Council. While this meeting was in progress, the officers waited in the adjoining room. These officers were the Lieutenant Governor, Home Secretary, Chief Secretary, Commissioner, Municipal Corporation of Delhi, Vice-Chairman, Delhi Development Authority, Senior Vice-President of the New Delhi Municipal Committee, and Inspector General of Police.

After the meeting with the members of Parliament, the officers were called in. The views of the members and other participants of the meeting were indicated by the Prime Minister. The general impression gathered was that slum and squatter settlements and non-conforming trade had to be removed but alternative accommodation was to be provided under Squatter Resettlement Scheme and such other approved schemes.

Actually, there was no fresh policy decision. The government decision, duly approved by the Union Cabinet, already existed; only the government's will to execute it speedily had been indicated. Similar meetings had been held by the Prime Minister earlier also. Two such meetings were held in July 1974. Besides the Minister of State for Works and Housing, Om Mehta, and Minister of State for Home Affairs, Ram Niwas Mirdha, these meetings were attended by Nirmal Mukerjee, Home Secretary, A.N. Banerji, Housing Secretary, P.N. Dhar, Secretary to the Prime Minister, Baleshwar Prasad, Lieutenant Governor, B.R. Tamta, Commissioner, Municipal Corporation of Delhi, Vijay Kapur, Deputy Commissioner, and myself. The Prime Minister expressed her unhappiness that effective action was not being taken against encroachments and illegal constructions. She wanted firm action to ensure that planned and balanced development of the city was brought about and environment were not degraded.

Following the above meetings under the chairmanship of the Prime Minister, Baleshwar Prasad reorganized the administrative machinery dealing with the encroachments and illegal constructions. In this connection, it is relevant to quote from the press report of 1 August 1974, apparently made by the reporter, A.R. Wig, after talking to the Lieutenant Governor:

> The Lt. Governor has reorganised the administrative machinery which deals to check racketeering in land. The revamping of the administrative machinery follows complaints of unauthorised construction and encroachment on a large scale by strong vested interests.
>
> The reorganised machinery has been directly placed in the charge of the Vice-Chairman of the DDA, Mr. Jagmohan....
>
> The DDA during the past fortnight has demolished 300 new constructions, including a large number of shops, commercial establishments, factories and pucca structures. In the trans-Jamuna area alone, the DDA cleared 200 acres of land which was in the process of being sold for construction purposes.
>
> The Lt. Governor has made it clear that racketeering in land should be curbed with a firm hand.
>
> He also plans to bring about close co-ordination between the DDA and the district authorities to tackle the menace.

From the above two meetings held in July 1974 and the action that followed, it should be quite clear that initiative had been taken at the highest level earlier also for dealing with the complex problem of squatting and unauthorized construction in Delhi. The impression that is being given to the Shah Commission that a sudden initiative was taken after the emergency is not correct. Unfortunately, no mention has been made about these two important meetings in the summary of the case, presented before the Commission, which seems to have been prepared on the basis of the report of the Jain Committee. In the summary, the figures of "clearances" for 1974 were also underplayed. The number was not 400, as given in the summary, but 7,000.

REINFORCEMENT OF THE POLICY

The government policy, programme and thinking on the subject was made clear and further reinforced by the subsequent statements made by the Prime Minister and the Minister for Works and Housing in Parliament and public, and also by the Chief Executive Councillor in the Delhi Metropolitan Council. Some of these pronouncements may be cited here:

(a) On 8 January 1976, the Prime Minister made a statement in the Rajya Sabha while intervening in the debate on the motion of thanks to the President for his address. The relevant portion of the statement as reported by the UNI and published by the *Times of India* is reproduced below:

> The Prime Minister today described the recent clearance of slums and squatters colonies as "not operation demolition but operation resettlement."

(b) In reply to a Parliament Question on 7 January 1976, the Minister for Works and Housing, K. Raghuramiah, told the Rajya Sabha that 29,563 residential squatters had been removed and resettled.

(c) On 15 January 1976, the Minister of State for Works and Housing, H.K.L. Bhagat, told the Rajya Sabha that "people were shifted by the Delhi Development Authority to distant places for resettlement purposes only. We are not removing people for the sake of fun."

(d) On 14 May 1976, Radha Raman, Chief Executive Councillor, hailed Delhi Development Authority's squatter plan. He, inter alia, stated:

> Delhi Development Authority's "Squatter Plan" during 1975-76 was the biggest peace time resettlement plan in any metropolitan area in the world. Presenting the Delhi Development Authority's budget for 1976-77 to the Metropolitan Council, Mr. Radha Raman said the Delhi Development

Authority had emerged as the biggest resettlement and development agency in Asia by developing 27 resettlement colonies with 80,000 plots to house about 4,00,000 squatters in Delhi.

Mr. Radha Raman said efforts had also been made for decongestion of the walled city of Delhi. The entire Jama Masjid complex was redeveloped to restore its ancient grandeur. About 1,000 squatters from the steps of the mosque were resettled, 462 junk dealers of the old Motia Khan junk market shifted to a new trading centre, 700 old motorpart dealers of Kashmere Gate, 320 wood merchants of Deshbandhu Gupta Road, 900 fruit and vegetable merchants of old Subzimandi had been resettled to give Delhi a cleaner and beautiful look. . . .

Mr. Radha Raman stressed that these steps, which seemed impossible for years, were made possible in a single year after the emergency.

(e) The Prime Minister herself made a surprise visit to the resettlement colonies. As reported in the *Hindustan Times* (10 July 76) and other leading papers, Indira Gandhi visited Khichripur, Mongolpuri, and Trilokpuri colonies and made personal inquiries about the condition of settlers. The *Times of India* (19 July 76) reported: "Mrs. Indira Gandhi today went round Khichripur, Mongolpuri and other resettlement colonies and met the people there. . . . She also planted some trees at the Trilokpuri colony."

(f) The programme of clearance and resettlement was also discussed in the Parliamentary Consultative Committee. In this connection, the relevant extract from the *Times of India* (28 August 1976) is quoted below:

The conditions in these colonies where Delhi's 1,25,000 families of squatter have been allotted plots came up for discussion in the Parliamentary Consultative Committee for the Ministry of Works and Housing today. . . .

Giving details of the progress, the Minister of State, Mr. H.K.L. Bhagat, informed the Members of Parliament that 200 km. of roads, topped with bitumen, had been laid. About 400 km. of brick-paved roads had also been constructed.

Besides, drainage, water supply and street lighting have been provided in the course of just eight months.

(g) Again at the time of laying of the foundation stone of 30 post offices in the resettlement colonies, H.K.L. Bhagat lauded the programme of the Delhi Development Authority and considered it unique. The following extract from the report of the *Hindustan Times* (15 November 76) is worth quoting:

> Mr. H.K.L. Bhagat, Union Minister of State for Works & Housing, said the resettlement of seven lakhs slum dwellers in a matter of months was a feat that had been accomplished only in Delhi. Many had criticised the scheme as unworkable and impossible. The success of "Delhi Experiment" may lead other states to emulate it.

The Planning Commission also recognized the advantage in clearing the public lands and resettling the squatters speedily. Radha Raman, Chief Executive Councillor, and I discussed the matter with P.N. Haksar, Deputy Chairman of the Planning Commission, and I.K. Gujral, Minister of State for Planning. A letter was also addressed on 17 February 1976 by Radha Raman to I.K. Gujral confirming the record of discussions and making formal request for additional allocation of funds. Subsequently, the Planning Commission and the Ministry of Works and Housing made larger funds available for the scheme.

It would be clear from the above that the DDA's programme of clearance-cum-resettlement-cum-development was carried out in accordance with the government policy, and in pursuance of the suggestion made by the Public Accounts Committee of Parliament. It had the concurrence of the Planning Commission. It was enthusiastically applauded by the central government and the Delhi Administration. A number of functions were held in the resettlement colonies which were attended by the Lieutenant Governor, ministers, and the other leading public men from time to time. The colonies were also visited by the members of the Parliamentary Consultative Committee attached to the Ministry of Works and Housing and the matter came up for discussion in the said Committee. Number of questions were tabled and answered in Parliament and the Delhi Metropolitan

Council. Thus, everything was done with the full knowledge and approval of Parliament and the government.

Nor was there any arbitrariness about the selection of the sites for clearance. No case was taken up without proper thought or consideration. For instance, the case of shifting of Cycle Market had been decided by the Supreme Court and, thereafter, clearance was taken up. Again, shifting of dairies was in consequence of the recommendations made by the Task Force constituted for dealing with the traffic problems of Shahjahanabad. There were a number of cases in which possession was required to be taken up by the Land Acquisition Collector under the Scheme of the Large Scale Acquisition and Development of Land in Delhi, sanctioned by the Government of India. Requests had also been received from the Tourism Ministry for clearance of the Dhaula Kuan site, from the Corporation for clearance of the Sarai Rohilla bridge site, from the New Delhi Municipal Committee for clearance of the "M" Avenue (Chanakyapuri), besides the requests from Delhi Electric Supply Undertaking, Delhi Transport Corporation, and from various government and semi-government organizations. Then, a number of Master Plan projects, such as redevelopment of Jama Masjid, relocation of Motia Khan, Iron and Junk Markets, Wood Market and other non-conforming trades were also pending.

There were complaints from public men also. For instance, Khurshid Alam, MP, wanted me to clear squatters and slum-dwellers around Jamia Millia. He wrote to me saying:

> You will please recall that we jointly inspected the unauthorised construction in July with the Jama Millia campus adjoining the Jamia Higher Secondary School. You will please also recall that after this joint inspection, you agreed that unauthorised construction of residential houses in the campus adjoining the main building of the institution was most undesirable and immediate steps were required to be taken to remove the unauthorised construction and ensure prevention of such construction in future.
>
> I have been receiving repeated reminders from the Vice-Chancellor, Jamia Millia, about this matter as they feel very strongly about it and naturally they are very apprehensive that slum conditions will prevail all over the campus if

immediate steps are not taken to remove the unauthorised construction and some positive steps are also taken to prevent further unauthorised construction in the area.

I would, therefore, request you to please initiate immediate action in this regard. . . .

Mulk Raj Anand, the noted writer and lover of old monuments, wanted clearance of area around Hauz Khas, particularly the tank and the site where Timur is understood to have camped in 1398. This is what he wrote to me on 12 September 1975:

> I feel ashamed to think that when other nations have built their cities, suburbs and villages all in 25 years, we cannot because of our democracy clear even a small slum in one of the most beautiful spots of Delhi, where the DDA has spent so much money.
>
> I only hope that you may be able to do something before the end of the year.
>
> All our welfare work is waiting for the Community Centre to be free of pollution, mosquitoes and germs. . . .
>
> I would like to give the last active years of my life to doing some social good. . . .

Acharya J.B. Kirplani, too, had been writing to the DDA and Delhi Municipal Corporation for getting a potter and a shack-dweller removed from a site adjoining his house. He was troubled by the nuisance to such an extent that he was even prepared to pay for the cost of removal. He, however, wanted the potter to be resettled at nearby vacant land. His suggestion could not be implemented because the plot suggested for resettlement was earmarked for green use and the shopkeepers in the neighbourhood of the potter were keen to occupy the site immediately after it was vacated by the potter.

Even those who critcize us severly for removing and resettling squatters and slum-dwellers sought our help, whenever it suited them. For example, in December 1976, Mahmood Qamar, Secretary of the Delhi Wakf Board, complained to the central government and the Delhi Administration against the Delhi Development Authority. He wrote:

> The Delhi Development Authority has removed squatters

from around the mosque on 22nd December, 1967 and has also demolished few structures from inside the mosque but did not touch the unauthorised structures carried out on them in floor of the mosque towards northern and southern sides, which are presenting ugly and slum conditions within the compound of the main mosque. The Delhi Wakf Board feels all-out clearance of the squatters from insides the mosque is imperative in the interest of this mosque of great historical importance.

The Delhi Administration is therefore, requested that the matter with regard to the clearance of the mosque from the squatters may kindly be taken up with the Delhi Development Authority. . . .

The DDA was able to responed swiftly to the requests of various departments because of the changed atmosphere. Once the confidence of the squatters had been won by speedy development and once realization dawned upon them that resettlement, with secure tenure, was in their interest, and the earlier they moved the better area they would get, a climate in favour of migration and resettlement was built up. We never pushed the squatters; we simply showed them the way—the way to better life, better future. The success achieved was astonishing.

Here, it may not be out of place to refer to Mao's advice to his partymen for dealing with the peasants. He said:

If you follow the course of not pushing the peasants, of trusting them, and of appealing to them in terms of their own material self-interest, you will again and again be astonished at the pace at which they will move in the directions which we hope for.

In such matters, moreover, it is the initial hesitation that needs to be overcome. Human beings are not very different from bees. As Tolstoy once observed:

No single bee moves unless the swarm rises. The swarm cannot rise, because one bee clings to the other and prevents it from separating itself from the swarm, and they all continue to hang. . . . All that is needed to change a solid mass of bees into a flying swarm, is for one bee to spread its wings and fly away, when the second, the third, the tenth and the hundredth will follow suit. . . .

No administration could have moved about seven lakhs people in one year without their consent. It was a movement, a trend, a successful manifestation of the policy of showing the way to better future.

Mrs Gandhi's Observation

Another reason for speedy clearance and development was the relegation of the politics of slums and discouragement to the pressure groups. In this respect, Indira Gandhi made some candid observations while addressing the All-India Congress Committee on 30 May 1976. She bluntly reminded her partymen that in the past the programme of slum clearance had not secured their support because of electoral considerations. She minced no words in telling them that their attitude of non-cooperation was anti-national. According to a report of the *Hindustan Times* (31 May 1976):

> Prime Minister Indira Gandhi today defended the city planning work taken up in Delhi recently and said there was bound to be hardship to some people.
>
> She told the A.I.C.C. that to plead that because there had been some inconvenience we should not go ahead with the programme is an anti-national attitude.
>
> Mrs. Indira Gandhi said that slum clearance work taken up in Delhi after the Emergency had to be on a large scale because very little had been done before the Emergency. There was no cooperation from even Congressmen for this work earlier. They pleaded for postponement of such works on such grounds as election time, monsoon, hot weather and cold weather.
>
> Some of these programmes had not secured the support of the Congressmen because of electoral and other considerations. Whether, it was urban renewal or land reforms, there were always some who suffered. She had sympathy for them and taken steps to help them.

The Prime Minister pointed out that the responsibility for the implementation of such programmes was not that of officials only but of Congressmen and people generally.

The truth is that overpoliticalization of the slum issue was the bane of civic life, and behind the smoke screen of human considerations lay the fangs of vested interests. Had anyone been really solicitous of the welfare of slum-dwellers, some solid social work would have been done for them. In fact, except for political interest and lip sympathy, total indifference to the plight of the slum-dwellers marked the scene. In this connection, I may quote from my article on "Urban Homeless":

> During my long sojurn in the slum and shacks, I have come across thousands of people asking for a chance to live in human conditions and showing off their sores with the zest of a begger. Some implore, while others curse, show their fists and get hysterical. But it is neither their pleading, nor their curses, nor their swollen and disease-ridden faces, that have unduly worried me. It is the stony look of those who pass and do not blink; it is the spectale of indifference, casualness and superficiality which has worried and discouraged me and made me sceptical about the success of our efforts to get rid of slums and shacks.

What has really been done by those who have been swearing by the name of humanism and squatter's welfare? Practically, no new sanction for any improvement or development work has been given after April 1977, in any resettlement colony. Not an inch of metalled road or brick paved lane has been added. No new tubewell has been dug, no new water-borne latrines built, no new dispensary constructed, and no new community centre set up. On the other hand, thousands of demolitions (Appendix I) have been carried out without notice and without providing any alternative accommodation. In the resettlement colonies, even cleaning arrangements have gone away. Repairs and maintenance works have virtually stopped. No one bothers. Everybody talks. It is not the welfare of the squatters and slum-dwellers, but its politics, that interests them. Those who stood above small considerations and kept the interest of the city and the nation uppermost in their mind are now being ridiculed on behalf of those who displayed a callous disregard for civic sense and future of the city.

What did Mahatma Gandhi expect our local leaders to do? He wanted the Municipal Councillors "not to seek honours or indulge in mutual rivalries, but to have real spirit of service and convert themselves into unpaid sweepers and road makers and, above all, take pride in doing so." How ably and sincerely we are fulfilling the wishes of Mahatma by whose name we swear every day?

CHAPTER V

DEMOLITION OR DEVELOPMENT?

> In the past the great spirits of mankind, the great philosophers, the religious leaders, had a grander sense of mankind, an expansive view of time and space. We are reducing everything to the immediate. We must get out of this parochial view, see things in their entirety, and project our vision into the future.
>
> PECCI

Nothing could be farther from truth than to describe our clearance-cum-resettlement operations as "demolition" operations. The entire drive was development-oriented and not "demolition-oriented." Its massive development content created extensive and stable employment opportunities and helped in converting slums of despair and darkness into settlements of hope and light, where one could acquire a place under the sun and face the future with courage and confidence. One of the basic purposes of our drive was to provide infrastructural and environmental facilities in the new colonies and to subject the erstwhile slum-dwellers to new social and cultural influences and create an urge in them to stand on their own feet. "If I give a man fish, I feed him for one day; if I teach him to fish, I feed him for the life time," goes a Chinese saying.

HUMAN CONSIDERATIONS

Clearance was part of an overall development effort—an effort that had suffered badly due to pressure of vested interests. Even when funds were provided, schools were not built for years, roads and bridges were not constructed. Costs of development projects mounted. River fronts were uglified, natural landscape and ridges were damaged; and areas surrounding historical places were turned into filthy slums. All this happened merely because of the presence of a few squatters who, probably, themselves wanted to shift but were often prevented to do so by the pressure groups and vested interests.

The extent of the imbalanced approach would be evident from one example. An old property was acquired in 1965 for constructing a school building for children. Compensation was paid to the claimant. But the vacant possession was not secured merely because of the presence of 39 squatter families who were supported by a pressure group. Even after the provision of funds, the school building could not be constructed for eleven years. All this happened in the name of human considerations. Has any one cared to assess the suffering to which thousands of poor innocent children were subjected? They had to go to tented schools at considerable distance. They had to run the risk of crossing the busy highways. They had to face the cold biting winds of Delhi winter. In the summer season, an incredibly hot tent was their only protection from the scorching sun. During the monsoon, a wet sticking site was often the base of their class rooms. All this happened for eleven long years. How many children fell sick, or even died? Who cares to assess? What matters is the political considerations, the voting-disposition of the squatters. This is the face of our real humanism. It does not bother us if education of thousands of our little children is adversely affected, or their health and intellectual capacity is irrepairably lacerated. To our human eye, all this is invisible.

Areas cleared during and before the emergency fall into the following four broad categories:

   (*i*) The area needed for public projects and for execution of schemes connected with the provision of community facilities in terms of the Delhi Master Plan. Such areas would include areas earmarked for roads, bridges, schools, hospitals, parks and playgrounds, various public utilities, public housing, bus depots, etc.

   (*ii*) Areas earmarked as Master Plan "green" such as northern and southern ridges, and areas around historical places.

   (*iii*) Areas constituting road berms, embankments of nallahs, drains and rivers or otherwise unfit for human habitation or incapable of development without prohibitive cost.

   (*iv*) Areas earmarked for various commercial, industrial and warehousing schemes, in terms of the Delhi Master Plan or comprising clusters of squatters which are too small to be served with public amenities like tubewells and community latrines because of economics of scale.

I would cite one or two examples of each of the above category of cases to illustrate how clearance was totally in public interest. Construction of Underbridge "M" Avenue, Chanakyapuri, was considered absolutely necessary to meet the increasing demand of traffic between South Delhi colonies and New Delhi areas. The project, which formed part of the Delhi Master Plan, was first taken up for implementation in 1971, and its original cost was estimated to be Rs 59 lakhs. The work was, however, held up due to the presence of the squatters. When the squatters were cleared in 1976 and resettled in the resettlement colony of Dakshanpuri, the cost of bridge had gone up to Rs 120 lakhs. The contribution to be made by the railways also increased from Rs 27 lakhs to 53 lakhs. And it is not only the cost but also the additional burden on the rolling stock, additional consumption of petrol and diesel, additional time and energy in commuting longer distances that matter. It may be relevant to ask: can a poor country like India afford wastage of resources in this manner? Now that bridge has been constructed and squatters cleared and resettled at proper sites, not only uncertainity of the squatters had ended but also a vital traffic link established, providing convenience to thousands of commuters and saving their time and energy in reaching their destinations.

Likewise, construction of Sarai Rohilla Overbridge, for which Rs 2 crores were provided, was held up, after acquisition of land because of the presence of squatters and unauthorized construction. The project was delayed for about five years. This escalated the cost of the bridge, caused frequent traffic jams, held up buses and trucks for hours, resulting in huge wastage of national resources. In yet another case, a vital road linking Ring Road and Okhla Road was not completed for ten long years. Imagine the inconvenience to the public and loss of resources in the shape of increased travel time and cost of petrol and pressure on rolling stock. It was only in July 1975, that clearance could be carried out and link road completed.

The Southern Ridge is a gift of nature to Delhi, which helps in keeping the ecological balance. Its occupation by squatters and continuous cutting of trees depleted the natural wealth and caused serious environmental degradation. It was, indeed, paradoxical that on the one hand large public funds were spent on growing more trees, while on the other, even the existing trees were allowed to be cut. Obviously, the Southern Ridge could not be a permanent abode of squatters, and the earlier they were resettled at appropriate places, the better it was for them and for the general environment of the city. Similar was the case with many other recreational spots, gardens and parks.

There are certain areas which are not fit for human habitation at all. For instance, on the embankment of the Najafgarh drain, near Karam Pura, thousands of families were squatting. There was hardly any civic amenity. The drain at the point emitted highly offensive smell. To keep thousands of families, including small children, in such unhealthy environment was absolutely cruel. To persuade the families squatting in such areas to move to new resettlement colonies, where only 40 per cent of the area was utilized for building and the remaining kept open for community facilities, was not only an act of civic reform but also an act of compassion and love.

In an old and historic settlement like Delhi, important consideration has to be given to the architectural and cultural heritage of the city. To allow areas around such historical places to remain with squatters would involve risk of damage and ultimate extinction of the monument, and would also scare away tourists. As an illustration, the case of Purana Quilla and its adjoining areas may be cited. Here, there were hundreds of squatters, kabari shops, workshops, etc., which had submerged "Mazar-a-Baedil" and the durgah of the famous Muslim saint Tusi. The approach to the exhibition ground was uglified, the environment of Purana Quilla spoiled, and the waterway near the Fort polluted. Removal of squatters from this area restored the grace and grandeur of the monument and also provided an excellent recreational spot for the local community. Similar beneficial results accrued from shifting squatters from the areas around important historical monuments like Haus Khas, Tughlakabad, Jama Masjid, Kotla Ferozeshah, Phool-Walon-ki-Sair, Mohd. Pur Pahari, and Kalkaji Temple.

Squatters and unauthorized occupants have sometime to be removed for *reasons of security*. For instance, the old residents of village Manglapuri had to be shifted because their dwellings came in between the two main runways of Palam Airport. The proposal to shift had been pending for a long time and it was only after the hijacking incident that the security risk involved in allowing the occupants to continue at the site acquired urgency. Resettlement of such occupants is obviously justified. In this connection, the following report of the *Statesman* (19 January 77) may be quoted:

Delhi Airport Gets Rid of Village

Residents of Manglapuri, the village in the middle of Delhi Airport, are being moved to the DDA's Palam Colony. The first of the 300 families were moved on Tuesday morning. And with this one of the biggest headaches of Airport officials is coming to an end. The hazard of people living so close to a runway is obvious, but in view of the need for effective security at Airport, the removal of the village had become even more necessary.

Small and scattered clusters are not viable units. Requirements of economies of scale make it necessary that large resettlement sites should be created so that provision of community services, such as the tubewells, schools, dispensaries, post offices, public telephone booths, are made available at reasonable cost. Nor is it practical to leave some clusters and remove others. The clusters which are removed might nurse the feeling of being discriminated against, while the clusters that remain might attract further squatting and eventually get relocated at more distant sites.

Infrastructural Facilities

Another invisible merit of clearance-cum-resettlement programme is that the allottee gets a secure tenure and becomes certain about his future. This, coupled with the provision of infrastructural and environmental facilities, stimulates the allottee's instinct of saving for house, and creates an urge in him to put up pucca structure by cutting down expenditure on consumer goods or by meeting substantial cost of the structure by contributing his own labour or by raising a small amount of loan.[1] The acquisition of plot/house impels him to call his family members from the native place. He thus attains a stable family life which makes its own contribution to the peace, orderliness, and progress of the city.

In fact, if any housing programme for the urban poor, particularly the bottom 40 per cent of them, has ever to succeed in a developing country like India, it has to be linked with the effort to exploit the instinct of saving for the house. This exploitation would be possible only when infrastructural facilities are provided by the public authorities and a desire is created in the allottee to make his own contribution for putting up a substantial structure. Experience of Latin American countries shows that if public investment infrastructure is made to the extent of one million dollars, the response of the allottee in making their own investment in providing houses is of the order of four million dollars.[2] In Delhi, where earlier resettlement was carried out, 86 per cent of the allottees over a period of time were put in pucca or semi-pucca structures even when the loan facilities were not available.[3] With loan facilities now extended, it is likely that almost all the allottees, excepting those who have no desire to settle permanently in Delhi, will be put in a pucca structure.

LOANS AND EMPLOYMENT OPPORTUNITIES

In the resettlement of squatters, carried out before the emergency, no facility of loan was made available. To help the squatters in putting up a substantial structure and to facilitate full use of infrastructural and environmental facilities, special efforts were made to secure housing loans for the resettled families. Ultimately these efforts succeeded, and loan facilities were extended by the State Bank of India at very cheap rate of interest. Routine work was curtailed to the minimum and effective coordination between the bank and the DDA officers was brought about to extend this facility to as many families as possible. Up to May 1977, about Rs 8.3 crores had been disbursed as loan in the resettlement colonies and as many as 65,000 families had been benefitted by this provision.

In respect of employment opportunities, too, the DDA's programme had innovative features. The critics tend to ignore the following four basic factors:

(*i*) Employment opportunity cannot be an end in itself. It has to be viewed in the context of other important considerations of public health, safety and general environment of the city.

(*ii*) The programme was not only of clearance and resettlement; it had a massive development content. The scheme of clearance, resettlement, and development were integrated and formed part of an overall process which gave birth to new employment opportunities.

(*iii*) The programme diversified and stabilized the employment opportunities, and had the effect of making the process of migration from rural to urban areas development-oriented, instead of "service-oriented." In other words, the squatter became an active component of development and participated in the industrial, commercial, and civic growth of the city, acquiring new skill and improving his future prospects.

(*iv*) The clearance and resettlement programme has a self-corrective mechanism, and wages and facilities obtained and services rendered generally get adjusted in a short time.

The general belief is that the squatters squat at a particular site because it happens to be near their place of work and their shifting reduces their employment opportunities or increases their expenditure on travel. Apart from the fact that in a number of cases, this belief is not well based, it ignores many other valid considerations. The employment opportunity cannot be an end in itself. It may, in fact, be self-defeating. Squatting at unhealthy place, as is usually the case, may adversely affect the health of the squatter's family and reduce, if not permanently damage, his capacity to earn, and also strain his meagre income on treatment of sick family members. Moreover, infectious diseases contracted by squatters by residing at unhealthy places endanger community life and sap the productive capacity of the entire city.

Although the Squatter Resettlement Scheme, as sanctioned by the central government, envisaged shifting of all the squatters to the periphery of the city with a view to discouraging squatting, every effort was made by the DDA in selecting those sites which were nearest and which had large employment opportunities and also high employment potential. Resettlement and development were corelated, so that employment opportunities arising out of new development works could be taken advantage of by the allottees of the resettlement colonies. One can just imagine the employment potential of developing 27 new resettlement colonies, 1,45,000 residential and 10,000 shop plots, 500 parks, and planting five lakhs trees, and constructing 5,300 houses exclusively for the squatters, 250 km of roads, 200 km of main drains, 400 km of small drains, 60 tubewells, 650 culverts, 80 km of water lines, 14,000 permanent lavatory seats, 23 new dispensaries, ten higher secondary schools, and various other buildings.

Subject to the availability of land, the following criteria were adopted in selecting the resettlement sites:

(*i*) Employment opportunities already existing in the nearby localities, such as industrial areas, and the additional employment opportunities that would be available consequent to development projects in and around the colony.

(*ii*) Position of the resettlement colony in the overall development pattern of metropolitan region.

(*iii*) Relationship of the resettlement colony to the existing transport network as well as the network for the future.

It needs to be emphasized that the employment opportunities for the squatters have to be viewed not only in the context of public health, safety, and city design but also in the context of the gains which would accrue to the resettlers in the immediate future as well as in the long run. Although a few settlers may suffer for a short time, most others would gain in the immediate future and in the long run.

KHICHRIPUR-TRILOKPURI

As an illustration, I would take the case of Khichripur-Trilokpuri-Kalyanpuri complex. In 1976-77, about 25,000 families were resettled in this complex. The extent and range of employment opportunities made available, and the general development potential of the complex would be evident from the following facts:

(*i*) About 1,500 acres of land has been developed. The

cost of development involved is about Rs 4 crores. Out of this, an expenditure of about Rs 2.5 crores had been incurred on various development works within about a year's time. These works involved engagement of about 3,000 persons per day for one year. During the period of peak activity, about 5,000 persons were employed on these works. In fact, at that time, the required number of workers were not available from this complex and the labour had to be brought from other places.

(*ii*) Construction of building, such as of schools, super bazars, fair price shops, doctor's forum, Adult Literacy Centres, dispensaries, balbaries, etc., costing about Rs 65 lakhs, had also been taken up giving employment to about 500 workers for one year.

(*iii*) A large housing scheme, comprising about 10,000 houses, costing about Rs 40 crores had also been formulated for integrated development of the entire complex. Out of this, work was actually taken up on 2,088 MIG/LIG houses, costing about Rs 8 crores. This work is expected to be completed in about two years, and has created employment opportunity for about 20 lakhs labour days, i.e. about 3,000 persons for two years.

(*iv*) The NDMC had also taken up construction of about 700 houses, costing about Rs 2 crores. This project has created employment opportunity of about eight lakh labour days.

(*v*) The DDA had also taken up construction of 1,000 EWS houses in this complex at a cost of about Rs 40 lakhs, creating employment opportunity of about one lakh labour days.

(*vi*) A Cattle Dairy Farm has also been developed in this complex. The cost of this project is, including proposed construction of 108 cattle sheds, about Rs 2 crores. This scheme has also provided employment opportunity of about five lakh labour days.

(*vii*) Another source for large employment opportunity to the people of this area has been the NOIDA project just across the Hindon Cut Canal. It is understood that several crores of rupees have been spent by the UP government on this project during the first phase of construction giving employment opportunity to thousands of persons. In addition to the employment potential during construction, this project would provide permanent employment to thousands of families in the new industries coming up in this area.

(*viii*) Delhi Small-Scale Industrial Corporation was persuaded to construct four large sheds for work centres and vocational training for the people of the area. In addition to creation of the employment opportunity during the construction of the sheds, it has provided substantial employment opportunity to the people in the form of cottage industries.

(*ix*) Apart from the construction projects the DDA has given employment to about 700 persons from this area on various scavenging and maintenance works.

(*x*) With regular allotment and secure tenure and facilities of bank loans, there was a spurt of construction activity which either gave self-employment or generated employment for others for direct construction as well as for ancilliary works connected with such constructions. About 1,500 shop plots were also developed and allotted, giving self-employment to the allottees.

(*xi*) In addition to the expansion of the existing Mother Milk Dairy, two amitious projects were envisaged in the immediate vicinity of this resettlement complex. These projects were: (*a*) Fish and Meat Processing Plant; and (*b*) development of one thousand acres of industrial areas across the National Highway in terms of the provision of the Delhi Master Plan. (The employment potential of these projects can be assessed from the fact that the first project was estimated to cost about Rs 10 crores and the second project would have involved development and construction expenditure of Rs 69 crores.)

(*xii*) A large-scale programme of horticulture development was taken up with four objectives of (*i*) increasing employment opportunities; (*ii*) stabilizing soil and reducing the sub-soil water; (*iii*) upgrading the resettlement colony environmentally; and (*iv*) creating small woodlands to ensure ecological balance of future development. The extent of the work done in this respect can be judged from the fact that in this complex alone in about a year's time half a million trees were planted. Some of the liabilities were converted into

Demolition or Development?

assets. The low-lying area was dug and converted into a lake. This not only provided additional employment opportunities but also facilitated arrangement for drainage and creating recreational spot for future.

Another illustration of the above proposition is the removal of squatters from Rama Krishna Puram area and their resettlement in Shakurpur. Thousands of families were squatting at odd places and scattered clusters in Rama Krishna Puram. Their shacks had been built in a haphazard manner in the open land, embankment of nallah and road berms. The squatters in this area were resettled in the newly developed resettlement colony of Shakurpur which is located right on the Ring Road. In the Rama Krishna Puram area, most of the squatters were competing for a limited number of jobs, such as domestic servants. On the other hand, in the newly developed resettlement colony of Shakurpur, new employment opportunities of higher order were available. This colony is near the thriving industrial area of Lawrence Road. It is also quite close to the new wholesale fruit and vegetable market which has been shifted from the congested area of the city. Adjoining Shakurpur colony, there is also a big housing complex and the residential estate of the DDA in the Shalimar Bagh area which is coming up fast both with regard to development of land and construction of houses. All these factors have combined to give far greater employment opportunities to the resettlers than were available to them at the old site. Moreover, in the new jobs wages were higher and they are protected by law. The employees enjoy regular holidays. The resettlers and their families have bright prospects of acquiring new skills, improving their economic lot, and also getting additional employment opportunities with further development in the aforesaid industrial, housing, and commercial complexes.

The factor of adjustment is equally important. Those who wish to secure the services of "service personnel," say a domestic servant, should either be willing to provide accommodation, individually or by pooling, or pay higher wages. Squatting on public lands of such service personnel, as domestic servants, really involves hidden subsidy to the comparatively better class of people at the expense of the community and at the expense of the squatter who is condemned to lead a miserable life in a nearby shack or squatter settlement. Experience of Delhi shows that wherever such resettled squatters continue to work on the old job, they demand, and invariably secure, higher wages to make up for the additional expenditure on travelling.

In a number of cases, where more than one member of the family is employed, it so happens that if resettlement causes increase in distance which one member of the family has to cover to reach his place of work, it reduces the distance in the case of the other member. The cases of those employed in regular establishments such as government offices and public undertakings and companies are only marginally affected. They get house rent allowances and other benefits. They can generally afford to keep cycles or bear additional expenditure.

Distance, in a place like Delhi, should be measured in terms of time, not in terms of miles. Therefore, the existing as well as projected transport system was kept in view while selecting the resettlement colonies. Almost all the 27 resettlement colonies were located on the strategic and important highways. They are easily accessible and all the major bus routes serve them. Again, their population would make any commercial transport service viable.

From the above, it should be quite clear that criticism in respect of absence of employment opportunities is of general character. It ignores the larger and more significant considerations. The project of the type executed has no single aim; it is an integrated programme of clearance, resettlement, and development. It takes care for the present as well as the future requirements of the city. It makes the process of migration to the city development-oriented. The squatters need not confine themselves to such casual domestic services as cleaning utensils. New avenues and more secure base of employment are open to them with protection of law and benefits of labour legislation.

Procedures

Removal of squatters and their resettlement was not a new phenomenon experienced during the emergency. Depending upon the circumstances, large-scale clearance operations were also undertaken before the emergency and about 53,000 squatter families had been resettled in the resettlement colonies.

Demolition or Development?

The procedures and practices adopted during the emergency were exactly the same as were adopted before the emergency. The shifting took place through the motivational contact and inducement and by offer of alternative plot on regular basis in the newly developed resettlement colony with basic civic amenities of much higher order than were available at the old site, and with prospect of future improvement.

The squatters themselves made repeated requests to the authorities for shifting to the new resettlement colonies. The squatters of Rani Bagh and Saria Bhatta approached the DDA on a number of occasions for getting themselves shifted to the resettlement colonies. In the pre-emergency days, the question of invoking the provision of the Public Premises Act never arose in practice. Apart from the fact that incentives and inducements were sufficiently attractive for shifting, the squatters were aware that the Public Premises Act would merely cause them harassment, subject them to unnecessary litigation, and ultimately burden them with payment of heavy damages for the entire period of unauthorized occupation, without securing any legal claim for allotment of alternative plots and flats. It was this awareness, coupled with the attraction of regular allotment and better amenities, that prompted the squatters to shift voluntarily to new areas.

Practical difficulties, too, make it impossible to finalize simultaneously the eviction proceedings of all the squatters in a given area and thus obtain vacant possession of the entire chunk of land. Obviously, without the entire chunk being available, execution of development scheme is not feasible.

In some other cases, action was taken by the Executive Officer/Estate Officer of the DDA in terms of the legal obligation devolving upon him, under the Delhi Development Act, to demolish unauthorized construction done without getting a layout and building plan sanctioned. In all such cases, too, alternative accommodation was made available by the DDA although there was no legal obligation to give such accommodation.

Strict instructions had been issued by me to ensure that no avoidable inconvenience was caused to the squatters, even on the day of shifting. These instructions, issued at the time of commencement of the clearance drive, ran as under:

At each of the resettlement sites, very strong *kanats* and tents should be fixed so as to enable the evictees to stay there for the night in case they reach late at the site. The children and the old people should be given special accommodation in these temporary tents.

The Executive Engineers in charge of the resettlement sites will remain at the respective sites when the clearance is being done. They will ensure that the requisite facilities, particularly of water, electricity and public latrines are available. They should also ensure that brick and other building materials are supplied. The Superintendent Engineer concerned and the Chief Engineer should also visit the sites regularly. Every day the officers concerned with the clearance operation will report to me on telephone or in person depending upon the nature of problem being handled.

In fact, quite a few squatters squatted with a view to securing alternative plots, and when the offer came, they readily accepted it. Arrangement for free transport, with facilities to remove bricks, "chaddars," "sirkies" and other building material existed. The possibility of acquiring ownership rights and of securing bank loans at cheap rates of interest were two other major incentives for voluntary shifting to the new resettlement colonies during the emergency.

BULLDOZING WHAT?

For securing clearance of slum and squatter settlements, the DDA relied on liberal incentives and inducements. Technicality of law could never have helped the squatters in securing alternative accommodation. Practical considerations rule out adoption of any course other than the one adopted. The DDA has never used force. Only the land racketeer and those who exploited human misery were kept at bay. Allegations of bulldozing of "houses" are totally wrong. Only debris and ramnants of vacated structures were cleared with the help of the bulldozers. This is what was exactly done before the emergency. How were areas like Yamuna Bazar, Nizamuddin, Idgah, Kotla Feroz Shah, etc., cleaned? Why wrong end of the stick is now being deliberately picked? Why a different criterion is now being applied? Actually, it is only the hypocrisy, the ambivalence, the obscurantism, and the ignorance, both feigned and real, that has suffered at our hands. What has been bulldozed is not the slums but their politics, not the *jhuggi-jhonpries*, but the physical and mental diseases that they reared. Bulldozers were instruments of development, and not of demolitions. About 90 per cent of the sites cleaned were immediately levelled, cleaned and developed.

WORLD BANK'S SCHEME

The World Bank's scheme of "site and services" has often been commended and its adoption by developing countries advocated. What has been done in Delhi since 1967 in respect of squatter settlements is nothing but a form of this scheme. It will be no exaggeration to say that Squatter Resettlement Scheme of Delhi is a forerunner of the World Bank Scheme. The difference between the two is only superficial. What we have done is the relocation of squatters in areas where they could permanently stay. Obviously, it would make no planning, economic or financial sense to provide services at the sites which are required for widening of roads, construction of bridges, schools, hospitals, and public utilities, or which are part of the complexes of historical monuments, or which are environmentally unsuitable, or which are incapable of being developed without prohibitive cost, or which are otherwise required to be kept open to maintain the ecological balance and minimize the crippling effect of high densities which maime and stultify human personality?

To justify a particular theory, some scholars of the Latin American countries romanticize the spontaneous growth of "shanty towns" even when the conditions of living are horrible and relocation is called for on humanitarian as well as planning grounds. In Rio de Janeiro, there are a number of "favels" which are in swamps or on slopes. Adlai Stevenson, after a trip to Rio, was asked by his host, what would he remember most? He said, "Why don't you ask what I want to forget most quickly?" The host said, "What is it?" Adlai Stevenson replied, "Slums of Rio de Janeiro."

A city, like any other living organism, requires open spaces in the same manner as human body requires lungs for breathing fresh air and supplying blood to its tissues and keeping them in a healthy state. Without such spaces, the city will develop thrombosis and die a premature death, causing maximum misery to the poor and condemning them permanently to congested and suffocating slums. Pandit Nehru once remarked, "I do not mind a person living in the open like a vagabond or a gypsy. Nor do I mind a person living in the mud hut. But I have a horror of slums. I believe in no argument, economic or other, which is based upon the creation of slums."

A NEW PATTERN

In our resettlement colonies, we have evolved a new pattern of human settlement—a settlement which provides fresh air, light, pure water and greenery, which balances our needs and resources, and which narrows the gap between urban and rural living. It aims at low cost housing pattern and rich environmental and cultural facilities. The two factors that cost more, namely expensive building material and constructions through contractors and intermediaries, have been largely eliminated. The tradition of construction by the individual himself, with the assistance of local craftsmen, exists in India, and about 90 per cent of buildings throughout India, history shows, were put up without the sophisticated advice of professional architects and engineers. In our resettlement colonies, attempt has been made to revive, rejuvenate, and adapt this tradition and encourage the resettlers to build their own houses. Our job had been to provide healthy environment and assist in relieving the birth pangs of new settlements to the extent it is possible within our means and resources.

Instances are not lacking when, under compulsion of circumstances, individuals built accommodation for themselves in a short time. In Jordan, refugees from Palestine built a separate city for themselves, and in Athens, refugees developed a separate district with excellent domestic architecture. In Lima, Peru, about 100,000 slum-dwellers organized themselves into four groups and overnight established a new colony on the outskirts of the city, Ciudadde Dios, and constructed accommodation on a self-help and mutual aid basis for about 5,000 families, within a modern layout which they had themselves conceived. They would have provided accommodation for the remaining families in less than a week but for the stoppage of work by police intervention.

It is not being appreciated that our resettlement colonies hold a great potential not only for the economic improvement but also for the social uplift of the resettled community. Through these colonies, we could bring about a peaceful social revolution and improve the productivity of the nation. By concentrating efforts on these colonies, we could in one stroke eliminate superstition and conservatism, give new values to the people, and raise their general capacity to live and enjoy a meaningful life.

One way of achieving this objective would be to set up community development centres with television halls, libraries, dispensaries, theatres, etc., and persuade young men and women to undertake social work in those areas and make the residents feel that they are a part of a great and ancient nation and in shaping its destiny they have a role to play. A beginning in this direction had been made. In addition to the television-cum-community centres set up by the DDA, the Delhi Social Welfare Board established excellent "balbaries" in the resettlement colonies. Mrs Kishan Chand showed a great deal of interest and enthusiasm in this regard. I have no doubt that a handful of dedicated social workers could really transform the outlook of the entire resettled community by making use of the infrastructure provided by the DDA and without running from pillar to post.

The challenge before us is not only to evolve a new pattern of human settlement but also to reform force that govern the life of the people. The DDA or any other local authority cannot undo the wrong inherent in our social and economic imbalances. "To believe that a single organ of the body politic, the city, can be cured of the disease while the same deadly cells flow through the entire blood stream is to betray an ignorance of elementary physiology." If our efforts to evolve a new and healthy pattern of human settlements have to yield full results, humanism, love and justice must find a deeper place in our hearts. We must revive the best in our ancient tradition and culture and adopt what Eric Fromm has termed, "priorities of life," and not "priorities of death." We must stop measuring the greatness of our cities by the skyscrapers and imposing centres of trade and commerce, but by the extent they enable men and women to lead a happy and tension-free life.

The hard facts of migration and the context (see Chapter II) in which we have to function must be recognized. Henceforth, we should have only migrant colonies, and not squatter colonies. Predetermined sites with basic civic amenities should be earmarked and developed in advance for those who migrate to the cities, and no one should be allowed to squat in a haphazard manner at any place. The city's annual budget must provide for development of sites equivalent to the number of migrants.

The small "shelter units" put up on the sites will acquire dignity and charm of their own if a healthy environment is provided around them. The emphasis should therefore be on the provision of community facilities—cheap transport, water supply, and sewerage and a drainage system. It is in this field that the knowledge of modern science and technology needs to be applied to make available the basic amenities at minimum cost. What is, in fact, needed is an entirely new system of community services—a new community latrine, easy to clean and maintain; a new kitchen which can provide cheap and clean food to hundreds of people in a short time; and a new system of disposal of waste and maintenance of other services.

Suggestions on the above lines were made by me as far back as 1971-72 in the two articles—"Urban Homeless" and "A New Human Settlement"—published in the magazine section of the *Hindustan Times* (13 June 1971 and 14 May 1972). Unfortunately, they were never seriously considered or implemented. Now, when practically all the existing squatters have been properly resettled, it is time that fresh migrant should not be allowed to squat haphazardly and predetermined migrant colonies set up to accommodate them.

Another feature of DDA's project of clearance and resettlement is that it facilitates the introduction of new techniques—the techniques which will help in the environmental upgradation of the colonies and in converting some of our worst liabilities into valuable assets.

There are two basic problems of the squatter settlement—disposal of human waste and use of charcoal energy. Anyone familiar with the pattern of cooking in the resettlement colonies knows that a very inferior quality of wood and coal is used for cooking purposes. This causes nuisance of smoke which is highly injurious to health. To meet this problem, one way is to make available energy at a cheap rate by innovative devices, such as bio-gas. The human waste can be recycled to produce this gas. Likewise, the cow dung can be used for the same purpose. In some of the resettlement colonies like the Kalyanpuri-Trilokpuri-Khichripur complex, it was intended to try this experiment on a large scale. The bio-gas plants were to be set up, making use of cow-dung of the Ghazipur Cattle Resettlement colony. The gas was intended to be supplied in the first phase to the cattle resettlement colony itself and then to the nearby resettlement colonies of Khichripur-Trilokpuri. This would have solved the problem of smoke nuisance as well disposal of the cow-dung. Likewise, the use of human waste in making bio-gas could have resulted in solving the problem of disposal of human waste, of eliminating smoke nuisance, and of meeting the energy requirements in a hygenic way.

A technique similar to this has been recently recommended by the first-prize winning entry in the international competition (1976) organized by the International Architectural Foundation for securing the best solution in regard to the relocation of 28,000 families of slum-dwellers from Tando Foreshone, Manila Bay, to Dagat Dagatan. At the relocated site, a self-contained community is proposed to be resettled within a *barangy*—a community of 500 families. The *barangy* will have its own community energy centre and facilities of toilet, community lavatories, solar heating system, etc.

Our new pattern of settlement involves relocation of squatters from unsuitable to suitable sites in and around which employment potential is built and environmental considerations are given pre-eminent place.

RESULTS

What do the above facts show? Can anyone in good conscience deny that what we have done is development, and not demolition? What we heralded is a dawn, not a doom. We have converted our liabilities into assets, and laid the foundation for cleaner and better environment. "Show me your cities and I would tell you about the cultural aims of its people." Seeing our city with 1,400 insanitary and inhuman clusters before the clearance-cum-resettlement-cum-development drive, what impression about the cultural pursuits of the people could be formed?

CHAPTER VI

LIES, HALF-TRUTHS AND CONVENIENT CONSCIENCE

History rests on the beaten

In a society like ours, sapped by hypocrisy and ambivalence, search for truth is extremely difficult. Politics and prejudice strangulate whatever yearning the nation may have for truth. Publication of certain books and press reports after the emergency hardly leave any doubt about it. Unfortunately, calumny is like an oil spot which leaves traces even when it is washed.

The concocted story of Ranjit Hotel meeting, which was so extensively reported by the press and the authors of the books on the emergency, has already been mentioned by me in Chapter I. I will now deal with the lies and half-truths presented as facts to the public by them.

Kuldip Nayyar's book, *The Judgement*, makes references to the DDA in respect of two matters. One relates to the demolitions of the lawyers chambers in Tis Hazari and the other to "150 deaths in the Turkman Gate incident." Both the references are wrong. The DDA had nothing to do with the demolition of lawyers chambers in Tis Hazari or in New Delhi courts. So far as the Turkman Gate incident is concerned, it was, as explained in Chapter VIII of this book, caused by strong emotional reaction to the family planning campaign. The number of rioters killed was six. Five of them had come from distant localities. Only one belonged to Turkman Gate area and he, too, was not affected by the clearance operation.

In her book, *Two Faces of Indira Gandhi*, Uma Vasudev relied solely on hearsay evidence. She merely put within inverted comas what Inder Mohan told her. She did not try to locate any documentary evidence or check up the veracity of Inder Mohan's version from other sources.

Inder Mohan goes about as a social worker. He is prone to exaggerations, and coins imaginary stories to suit his ends. In a write-up in *Seminar* (June 1977), he deliberately gave a false figure of 300 dead in Turkman Gate incident, that is, 50 times the actual number!

Inder Mohan has tried to link me, Sanjay Gandhi, and Jama Masjid clearance by referring to the estimates of Rs 1.80 crores for the construction of a shopping complex in Painwala. I cannot say anything about Inder Mohan's discussions with Sanjay or his arrest. So far as Inder Mohan's story relating to me is concerned, it is false and imaginary. He says, and Uma Vasudeva quotes him faithfully, that the figure of Rs 1.80 crores was mentioned by me as well as Sanjay Gandhi. The facts are that no project with any architectural and engineering drawings and other details had been formulated. The question of preparing any financial estimates, without any basic drawings and data, could never arise. The extent to which imaginary stories have been coined by Inder Mohan, and used by Uma Vasudev would be evident from her reference to Inder Mohan's meeting with me on 19 September 1975 in my "spacious office" on the eighteenth floor of Vikas Minar. She did not know that DDA's office shifted to Vikas Minar in July 1976, that is, about nine months after Inder Mohan's alleged meeting with me. Even after shifting to Vikas Minar, my office was on the fifth floor. Inder Mohan obviously relied too much on his imagination.

Inder Mohan's hostility to me could be partly due to misunderstanding and partly to his frustration. For some time, Inder Mohan was friendly to me, and I thought that he was genuinely interested in the social welfare work in the Jama Masjid area. He even persuaded me to give him a short-term job in the DDA. But after some time, I was given to understand that Inder Mohan was trying to build, for personal and political reasons, a pocket of influence amongst the shopkeepers of Jama Masjid complex. He and his friend, Siraj Piracha, started using my name for the purpose. Two prominent local leaders and a group of shopkeepers protested to me. I thought it prudent to keep Inder Mohan and Siraj Piracha at distance. I had also started asking the question: if Inder Mohan was really interested in genuine social work, why was he confining himself to petty politics of a few shopkeepers of Jama Masjid staircases alone, particularly when some local leaders had started accusing him of political ambitions and doubting his bonafides after February 1975 riots in Jama Masjid? Why did he not move to various squatter settlements where there was a much greater scope for doing social work?

All these developments seem to have annoyed Inder Mohan, and explain his attitude of hostility. He has, moreover, a vested interest in justifying all the false and exaggerated stories he has been circulating to his friends in the press. He and Siraj Piracha were seen in the Commission premises tutoring and prompting witnesses from Turkman Gate and Jama Masjid area. They did everything possible to demoralize and defame me.

Taking advantage of the vitiated atmosphere and knowing fully well that I had no access to the press to refute his false and frivolous allegations, Inder Mohan published a highly scurrilous article against me in *Mainstream*. The ostensible objective was to create prejudice against me in the minds of persons in authority. He also accused me falsely for demolishing Kalan Mahal, supposedly a historic building where Shahjahan is rumoured to have stayed. The building was not a protected monument. It was in total ruin and in occupation of squatters. It was acquired in 1965 by the Directorate of Education, Delhi Administration, for constructing two new school buildings at the site. The prejudice of Inder Mohan impelled him to accuse me even for the decision which the Delhi Administration took as far back as 1965. All that the DDA did in the matter was to provide alternative accommodation to the slum-dwellers and squatters who were precariously perched against the crumbling walls of the dangerous and dilapidated buildings.

The fact that even elementary care has not been taken to ascertain the correct position is also evident from what Uma Vasudev writes about my award. She says, "His controversial role during the emergency finds an ironical twist in the fact that he was awarded the Padma Shri for his 'significant contribution in the formulation and implementation of the Delhi Master Plan, for playing a pioneering role in the planning and implementation of their development projects, and for breaking new grounds in the matter of slum clearance'." This award was given to me not in emergency, but on 26 January 1971.

Mankekar's book, *Decline and Fall of Indira Gandhi*, contains, besides the concocted story of Ranjit Hotel, stories based upon Inder Mohan's false and slanted versions. Mankekar also made some reckless statements. Without giving any details, he says, "Hundred of them [squatters] fell sick and died." I can assert with confidence, and on the basis of records, that not a single person died due to shifting. From the comparison of the conditions prevailing in the pre-resettlement sites and the resettlement colonies, made in Chapter I, it would be clear even to the most prejudicial observer that environment of the latter were far more conducive to healthy living than those of the former.

The manner in which scant respect has been shown to the facts would also be evident from the superficial observations of Mankekar about Munirka lands. He says, "They [the landowners] were paid compensation at the rate of Re 1 or Rs 1.50 per square yard. The Delhi Development Authority later charged Rs 100 to Rs 150 for the same land." The facts are that the undeveloped land was acquired by paying compensation determined by the courts on the basis of market value prevailing at the time of notification, and two bed-room flats, with a separate living and drawing room, kitchen, bath, lounge and a verandah were allotted to the individuals in the middle-income group at price ranging from Rs 40,000 to Rs 45,000. This included the cost of development of land, provision of municipal services, and community facilities like parks and school sites, and construction of the flat itself. In fact, the boot is on the other leg. Whereas the allottees of the DDA flats are paying about Rs 400 per month as hire-purchase instalment, the prevailing rent in the locality is Rs 600 to Rs 700 per month. In other words, the allottees are virtually earning a premium of Rs 200 to Rs 300 per month without undergoing any trouble that a private house builder has to face in Delhi. This is a classic illustration of the fact that, in our set-up, those who try to solve some basic social problem get brickbats, while those who sit back and do nothing either get away with their indolence and lack of initiative or at the most get a mild, casual, reprimand of a general nature. Incidently, Mankekar himself is a beneficiary of the land allotted to the Cooperative Societies on no-profit-no-loss basis.

Delhi Under Emergency is another book in the same genre. It claims to give an exhaustive, "blow by blow" account of the Turkman Gate incident. But actually it ignores the background as well its vital aspects. It is more fanciful than factual. It speaks through persons specially "selected" to say what the authors had already decided to write. For instance, they present a very dark picture of Mangolpuri Resettlement Colony through one Dwarka Prasad. Yet this is the colony which elected the Congress candidate in the Municipal Corporation elections of June 1977 with overwhelming majority, when most of the other constituencies voted against the Congress. I am not concerned with the Congress victory or defeat. All that I wish to demonstrate is that the account of John Dayal and Ajoy Bose about the conditions of living in the resettlement colony of Mangolpuri is false. Had the conditions been so bad as the authors point out and the resettlers so bitter as they want us to believe would they have voted so enthusiastically for Sajjan Kumar, Congress candidate, particularly when he had wholeheartedly supported the clearance-cum-resettlement drive? The truth is that the squatters, who were previously living in utter misery in scattered clusters with practically no civic amenities, were overwhelmed by the benefits of resettlement and development and expressed their gratitude in no uncertain terms.

Dayal and Bose have also made naive observations about DDA's role and functions in regard to implementation of the Master Plan and the development schemes envisaged under it. I am convinced that like other authors, they have not made even elementary study of the subject. The task assigned to the DDA was not merely housing, as Dayal and Bose assert, but to secure planned development of the capital. The residential, industrial, commercial, "green," and institutional components of the plan have been earmarked under the statute, and the DDA had not developed any commercial slant. It had auctioned, as it had been auctioning since 1962, commercial sites. So far as residential land is concerned, no more than one per cent has been sold through auction restricted to those who have no other plot or house in Delhi. The remaining 99 per cent residential land has been disposed of at fixed rate, worked out on no-profit-no-loss basis.

Michael Henderson's book *Experiment with Untruth* is another untrue account based upon the version of story-teller, Inder Mohan, who is the common denominator of all the exaggerations and falsehood.

David Selbourne, author of *An Eye to India*, goes still further. Acccording to him, 25,000 people are understood to have suffered in the suburban relocation for which compulsory sterilization was a pre-condition. All these observations are based on rumours and not on facts. Not in a single case, compulsory sterilization was made a pre-condition for allotment of land or plot to those who were affected by the clearance-cum-resettlement operations. Some additional incentives were provided for the family planning campaign of the Delhi Administration but in no case allotment of alternative flat or plot was denied to a person who was covered by the DDA's clearance-cum-resettlement operation.

It is, indeed, shocking that none of the writers of the Turkman Gate story makes it clear that the area had been declared unfit for human habitation as far back as 1938, that the houses in question were dangerous and dilapidated and had been acquired during 1948-52, that, as was tragically demonstrated by eight subsequent deaths due to the house collapses, inmates lived under constant risk of death, and that against 120 houses cleared about 1,000 alternative allotments had been made—200 flats in a most attractive colony of Ranjeet Nagar (Patel Nagar) and Shahdara to bonafide slum-dwellers, and 600 residential plots and 200 commercial plots to the squatters in the resettlement colonies. How unfair it is that no one speaks of the compensation, of beautiful flats, or of liberal terms of allotment of plots and commercial sites, the market value of which would run into several lakhs. Everyone speaks of bulldozers although they were used, as they have been used for the last decade or so, for clearing the debris or structures vacated by the previous occupants who usually take all the salvageable building material on the trucks provided to them free of cost by the DDA. What the authors of emergency books have written is not history, not even instant history, but a hasty, prejudiced, careless, and one-sided version salted and spiced by sensationalism. To knowledgeable persons, their account, to use Gandhi's description of Katharine Mayo's book, *Mother India*, is like a "gutter inspector report." It deliberately ignores the positive aspects, and shows little respect for intellectual honesty. The authors may by their own queer sense of justice hold some people guilty. But what about the verdict of history? Will it not be terrible for them? When the haze and dust of ignorance and prejudices have died down, the faces of those really guilty of suppression of facts and giving slanted or twisted version would stand exposed.

Let alone the journalists and writers who have created false impression on the public mind, the depositions so far made by some of the erstwhile persons in authority betray a total lack of commitment to truth and justice. The statements made by them before the Commission are truly amazing. They contradict the written records and their own public pronouncements made in Parliament or to the press or on radio and television. They have pursuaded themselves to believe that the easiest way for them to escape responsibility for the alleged lapses or excesses was to feign ignorance and to pass on the blame either to their seniors or their juniors. Unwittingly, they are admitting what poor stuff they were made of. They went on doing things against their conscience or belief without lodging slightest protest or stating their point of view in writing, or seeking leave, transfer or retirement.

Kishan Chand, former Lieutenant Governor, told the Commission that he was merely an innocent spectator, while four or five officers who had direct access to the Prime Minister "ruled" the city. Nothing could be further from truth than this statement. If any officer was responsible for the alleged emergence of a new power structure in Delhi, it was Kishan Chand. He bullied and pressurized the officers who wanted to work within the limits of administrative proprieties or argue their point of view forcefully.

Kishan Chand hardly made any secret of the manner in which he proposed to function as Lieutenant Governor of Delhi. Soon after assumption of office, he publically declared that he was a humble soldier of Indira Gandhi and had taken up the job to serve her. This declaration betrays his mental attitude and his general inclination to flatter or please the persons in authority. A few days before the emergency, he openly organized deployment of Delhi Transport Corporation buses for transporting people to the rally outside the Prime Minister's house. A press report of 20 September 1975 stated, "the true follower [of Mrs Indira Gandhi] has virtually converted Raj Niwas to the office of Delhi Pardesh Congress Committee; even the junior officers say that Shri Kishan Chand is lowering the dignity of the office of Lt. Governor."

Kishan Chand even tried to victimize me for not allowing officials of the DDA to join the rally. He was anxious to have a massive rally staged and create what Nawin Chawla described to the Commission a *lahar*, a wave, a movement, in favour of Indira Gandhi. When Kishan Chand learnt that I had told my Special Assistant to get the staff intending to go to the rally marked absent, he got very annoyed. Soon thereafter, he moved the Ministry of Works and Housing for my transfer, although the Appointment Committee of the Cabinet comprising Prime Minister, Home Minister, and the Housing Minister, on the recommendations of all concerned, including the Cabinet Secretary, had approved of my continuance for another year. A month or so earlier, the ESCAP, UN organization for South East Asia Region, had enquired from the central government whether my services could be made available to them for a period of three months for preparing a report. On receipt of this query, A.N. Banerji, Secretary, Ministry of Works and Housing, asked Kishan Chand whether I could be released for a period of three months. He replied, "what to speak of three months, I cannot spare him for three days." Yet, such was Kishan Chand's regard for principles and administrative propriety that as soon as he came to know about my attitude towards the rally, he moved for my transfer and suggested for appointment the name of U.S. Sirivastava who was reported to have helped in the deployment of Delhi Transport Corporation fleet. Since, however, this was a lower level intrigue and I could not be transferred without the approval of the Appointment Committee of the Cabinet, the move fell through.

As indicated elsewhere in the book, there was nothing wrong in the programme of clearance and resettlement of squatters or shifting non-conforming trade and industry. This was not only in accordance with the policy of the government approved long ago but also in the overall interest of development of the city. But as the programme began to be subjected to criticism and as the Enquiry Commission was set up, Kishan Chand, for reasons known to him, started feigning ignorance and circulating the story of being an "innocent spectator." Actually, it was he who initiated the drive by personally ordering the massive "demolition of old Subzimandi" area in the first week of July 1975 while I was in Australia. He was also responsible for approving the demolition of lawyers chambers in the District Courts.

Kishan Chand presided over a number of public functions organized in the resettlement colonies, and warmly eulogized the drive of clearance and resettlement. He himself visited the Turkman Gate area twice. Soon after the Turkman Gate incident, he passed the orders on the files relating to the clearance of Sarai Khalil and Gali Khan-i-khana area and acquisition of some private properties in these localities. He aslo visited with me Sarai Rohilla Resettlement complex where families from Sarai Khalil were accommodated. He obtained special notes from me on the subject for incorporating them in his speech for the Governors' Conference and his annual address to the Delhi Metropolitan Council. He presided over almost all the meetings of the DDA in which various decisions connected with the clearance programme were taken. In some cases, such as the case relating to change of land use of Turkman Gate, he personally took the decision after the DDA had resolved to leave the decision to him. On a number of occasions, and mostly without any justification whatsoever, he appeared on the television or gave a brief talk to the radio praising the programme. He even asked Nawin Chawla to get a film made on the subject. The script of the film, inter alia, read that under the overall direction of the Lieutenant Governor an integrated programme for resettlement work was brought about. That Kishan Chand was prone to assume power, which did not vest with him, would be evident from the orders issued by him in February 1976, requiring that, in future, plots, flats or shops would be allotted only to those who had restricted their family by undergoing sterilization. He wanted these orders to be implemented without making any reference to the Government of India.

Notwithstanding all these facts and connected evidence, Kishan Chand stated before the Commission, without any hesitation, that he was merely a "spectator" and that Raj Niwas was a deserted place "in which not even dogs barked." For this statement, hardly any precedent can be found in the history of administrative set-up. Kishan Chand wanted the Commission to believe that if he had passed written orders, he did so merely to fulfil the statutory obligation, and if he gave oral orders or approval, he had been ignored. What was the necessity of anyone ignoring him when he would have signed the file in any case? This contradiction in his stand would not occur to him. In fact, Kishan Chand, without any compunction of conscience or regard for elementary fairness, adopted the attitude: "head I win, tale you lose."

The posture adopted by Tamta before the Commission is equally amazing. A sudden realization seem to have dawned upon him that clearance or demolition was something of an evil to which he was drawn under the threat of Maintenance of Internal Security Act. Nothing could be more untrue or hypocritical. Tamta's stand is wholly contradicted by his attitude and behaviour before the emergency and also by the documentary evidence and his voluntary statements during the emergency.

It is a matter of common knowledge that Tamta belonged to the new emerging class of officers who relied more upon their political or what they considered popular posture than on their ability. Short-term gain was considered more important than long-term interests of the civic administration and planned development of the capital. He was appointed Commissioner of the Delhi Municipal Corporation against the wishes of the Mayor and the Lieutenant Governor. Soon thereafter, he let it be known that he had joined the Corporation to finish the Jan Sangh. This is exactly what happened. The Corporation was superseded. Tamta became the sole administrator, enjoying vast powers of the deliberative and executive wings.

Tamta's deposition to exceed the set norms of administrative propriety was evident even before the emergency. A press report of 19 June 1975 clearly reveals that Tamta was present in the crowd outside the Prime Minister house, an area outside the jurisdiction of the Corporation, and was seen shouting slogans. Was he afraid of Maintenance of Internal Security Act at that time, too? On 14 December 1975, Tamta joined, as is indicated by the press reports of that day, birthday celebrations of Sanjay Gandhi. Would he have been punished had he not joined the birthday celebrations? Those like me who kept aloof from such meetings were not persecuted.

What Tamta started voluntarily during the emergency is equally revealing. It demonstrates to what extent he is capable of volte-face. He was fond of holding press conferences regularly and issuing press notes. In one such press note, Tamta claimed that in the matter of removal of encroachments, the Municipal Corporation of Delhi had taken a lead in the country. Another press note of 24 July 1975 announced that "in the biggest ever clearance operation, the demolition squad of the Delhi Municipal Corporation went into action against 700 unauthorised establishments at Tilak Nagar Chowk." Likewise, the press note of 2 January 1976 stated that, "in a major clearance operation in the rural zone, about 200 unauthorised shops and encroachments on public lands were demolished near village Samalkha and Kapeshera." In respect of clearance from the staircase of Jama Masjid, it was the Corporation which took the action. In the two press notes issued by the Corporation it was, inter alia, stated that this operation was personally supervised by Tamta, Commissioner, and K.N. Sharma, Deputy Commissioner, Municipal Corporation. I would, however, like to dispel the impression that the DDA is trying to shelve its responsibility. The correct position is that the major role in regard to the redevelopment of Jama Masjid area was played by the DDA. All that I am trying to clarify is that, so far as the clearance from staircases, and pathways/passages is concerned, it was the legal responsibility of the Corporation to take action, and the Corporation did so.

In June 1976, a Coordination Committee comprising Chief Secretary, Delhi Administration, Deputy Commissioner, representatives of the Home Department of the Delhi Administration, Delhi Police, the Municipal Corporation, the Delhi Development Authority and the New Delhi Municipal Committee was constituted. All important decisions were taken by this Committee. In the meeting of the Committee held on 25 May 1976, Tamta pointed out that there were about 25,000 *jhuggies* within the local jurisdiction of the Corporation and urged that the DDA should be asked to shift them to its resettlement colonies. On this request of Tamta, the Coordination Committee decided to bring the matter to the notice of the Vice-Chairman immediately and advise him to take necessary steps to shift the squatters. Again, in the meeting held on 10 June 1976, Tamta indicated, in response to a query from the Chief Secretary, that although the slum clearance work had been transferred to the DDA, the

Chawri Bazar Scheme would be handled by the Corporation and also financed by it. Tamta stated that the scheme had been explained to the public and there were no repercussions.

The above two instances clearly show that officers like Tamta not only actively participated in the meetings but also took initiative to get the clearance done. Now it is these very officers who want the Commission to believe that they were pressurized to do certain things, and what is still more morally reprehensible, other officers were responsible for what happened.

The attitude of officers like the Chief Secretary, Deputy Commissioner, and the Inspector-General was not very different. They actively participated in the decision-making process and supported the various measures taken. In a number of cases, they even pressurized the DDA to carry out clearance on priority basis. For instance, in 33 cases, the Secretary of Lands and Building Department of the Delhi Administration of which the Chief Secretary is in overall charge pressed the DDA hard for immediate clearance of the sites. Likewise, the Chief Secretary was keen that the scheme to clear Mangolpuri village and lands near Milan Cinema should be speedily executed.

I wish to make it clear to the Commission that by citing the above instances I am not implying that I was not associated with the decisions or that anything wrong was done in clearing areas and resettling squatters in the manner it was done. All that I am trying to emphasize is that it is both administratively and morally wrong on the part of other organizations and senior officers to disclaim total responsibility. This reflects not only on the quality of their deposition before the Commission but also on the nature of commitment they had to their work.

In his deposition before the Commission, Mohsin, Deputy Minister, Home, in Mrs Gandhi's Cabinet, adopted an attitude critical of the DDA and stated that he went to the Turkman Gate on 23 or 24 April 1976 and met the Deputy Commissioner (Slums), H.K Lal. He did not make it clear to the Commission as to why he did not get the work stopped if something wrong was going on, or why did he not speak to the Home Minister or Minister of Works and Housing. Evidently, he either did not think anything wrong was being done or lacked courage of conviction to say what he really felt and thought.

Mohsin also told the Commission that President Fakhruddin

Ali Ahmad was unhappy. His unhappiness, in fact, was due to the wrong picture presented to him. Towards the end of May 1976, H.K.L. Bhagat, former Minister of State for Works and Housing, and I met the President. He was in a relaxed mood. With grace and charm peculiarly his own, he talked informally. I explained to him what had been done in Jama Masjid complex and what was proposed to be done further. I also showed to him a few photographs. The President was visibly happy over the delightful environment created around Jama Masjid and himself spoke of the significant improvement that had been brought about around the historical mosque of Idgah where Aurangzeb used to say prayers. The President had himself been performing his annual Id prayers in Idgah, and was full of praise of the garden and the lawn which the DDA had developed after clearing the junk shops and stores. The President expressed the hope that the visitors to Jama Masjid would not now see the slums and insanitary conditions which previously prevailed in the area.

Apparently, the President had not been correctly informed about our allotment scheme. He seemed to have been given the impression that shopkeepers had been sent miles away. I informed the President that all the shopkeepers had been accommodated in the 350 shops built in Urdu Bazar in the Jama Masjid complex itself, and that only workshops, lathes, and factories which had no real link with the Jama Masjid complex, either by way of cultural heritage or by way of conforming industries, had been allotted alternative sites in the newly developed complex in Mayapuri, where thousands of industrial and warehousing units had been shifted from Motia Khan iron merchant market and Idgah spare parts and kabari markets. I also told the President that a number of persons carrying out work around Jama Masjid on "teh bazari" licence of about 3 or 4 sq. yds. only had been given plots of hundred sq. yds. in Mayapuri, where the average price at the time of allotment was Rs 1,000 per sq. yd. In other words, each of the allottee had got a plot worth Rs 1 lakh. If the allottees took initiative and made use of the valuable allotments made to them, they could definitely carve out a bright future for themselves and their children. In Jama Masjid complex, they were condemned to perpetual misery with no scope for future improvement. They had only temporary licence of 3 or 4 sq. yds. and were at the mercy of the local body. All these revelations came as a surprise to the President. No one had given him the facts.

In respect of the Turkman Gate area, too, I explained the entire background of the case which apparently had been kept away from the President. I told him how the scheme of slum clearance had been conceived as far back as 1938, how the properties had been acquired in 1948-52, how the dilapidated and dangerous houses were collapsing, how the occupants were living under fear of death, how the Corporation Resolution had provided for allotment only to the old slum-dwellers, how the DDA had liberalized these provisions and made allotments even to the squatters and fresh entrants, and how against 120 houses cleared about 1,000 alternative allotments, including 200 flats in Ranjit Nagar (Patel Nagar) area, 400 residential plots and 200 commercial plots had been made. The President was rather surprised that no one had told him either about the commercial allotment or about the Ranjit Nagar flats.

The President made pleasant remarks about the manner in which the DDA had carried out the shifting in Sarai Khalil area. He also talked about the general scheme of redevelopment of Shahjahanabad and desired to know as to what happened to the recommendations made in my book about reservation of the entire land in Mata Sundri Road complex for building second Shahjahanabad. H.K.L. Bhagat informed the President that he was taking special steps to ensure that the land in question was made available for purpose. The President wanted Bhagat to keep him informed about the progress in the matter.

These facts may be kept in view while evaluating the evidence of Mohsin and others who have referred to the alleged unhappiness of the President.

It may be interesting to refer to the brief talk which I had with Khwaja Ahmed Abbas, a noted writer, at a dinner at a common friend's house in early 1976. I had not met Abbas earlier, but was aware of his progressive views. In the casual conversation, he made a critical reference about the shifting of some as the Jama Masjid area *kabaries* to Mayapuri. I replied to Abbas somewhat in these words, "Knowing your views, I thought you would

Lies, Half-Truths and Convenient Conscience

appreciate what had been done. How would it serve the cause of the poor if the *kabaries* were condemned in perpetuity to a small *takht*, a *Teh-Bazari* of a few feet. Now, they have got a plot of 100 sq. yds. each, worth Rs 1 lakh. They have skill. They work hard. But they could not improve their lot at the old site as they had limited space and were always at the mercy of a few exploiters. Now, at the new sites in thriving industrial and warehousing colony in Mayapuri, they have new avenues, new opportunities, to carve out an independent and bright future for themselves and their children. All that is required is extricating the poor from the narrow grooves of obscurantism." "Who will do that"? This is all Abbas could say before the conversation was interrupted by another friend. The real problem is to prevent the poor from becoming a victim of propaganda.

Unfortunately, even in respect of cases of relocation for the benefit of the allottees, communal slant is being given by vested interests. How unfair this accusation is can be seen from the fact that the DDA has spent over Rs $1\frac{1}{2}$ crores in the redevelopment of Jama Masjid complex and another Rs 80,000 in renovation of two mosques in Turkman Gate. In fact, at one stage, I was accused of giving special benefits to the people of Jama Masjid and Turkman Gate area, while denying similar benefits in other localities. These people who are now making charges of communal slant and circulating false stories like that of "Ranjit Hotel" and "second Pakistan" would do well to go through my book *Rebuilding Shahjahanabad: The Walled City of Delhi* which is nothing but an impassioned plea for the revival of healthy components of Mughal culture.

A few "experts" like S.A. Shafi, who have no practical experience of any fieldwork and who cannot show even a single layout which has been actually implemented and in respect of which there is an encouraging feedback, have found an excellent opportunity to denigrate the DDA. According to them, it is a violation of the Master Plan to remove the stall holders, hazardous and non-conforming trades, such as foundries and welding shops, from the staircase of Jama Masjid and to accommodate the conforming trades in the 350 shops built, in continuation of the shops earlier constructed, in the Meena Bazar. At the time of earlier construction, no one alleged violation of land use.

Now, violation of land use plan is being alleged by these experts. If there is any violation in principle, it is immaterial whether the violation relates to a smaller number or a larger number of shops. What is still more astounding is that violation is being alleged when green space has been added around Jama Masjid. Shafi told the Commission about his objections and all that he had stated to Bhagwan Sahay, Chairman, Urban Arts Commission, about DDA's lawn around Jama Masjid and Meena Bazar Shopping Complex, but he chose to suppress the most material point—Bhagwan Sahay's approval of the lay-out of the lawn and Shopping Complex.

Shafi also alleged violation of the Master Plan in the establishment of resettlement colonies at periphery of the present urban limit. He is unaware that such colonies were established during 1967-69 in accordance with the decision taken by the Ministry of Works and Housing of which TCPO is a part in 1967 with the consent and concurrence of all leading political parties. The colonies like Hatsal and Nangloi were set up at that time. Shafi has probably never gone out and seen those colonies or has found it convenient to ignore their existence. Nor is it clear as to where additional population can be accommodated, if the population has increased much beyond what was projected in the Master Plan.

Shafi has also spread wrong information about drainage of the areas on which resettlement colonies have been developed. He has not cared to ascertain facts. The trans-Yamuna colony of Khichripur-Trilokpuri has been a special target of his attack. The actual position in regard to this colony was explained in the meeting of the Coordination Committee, held on 7 June 1976. In this meeting, the Chief Engineer of the DDA indicated that the trans-Yamuna area was expected to accommodate a population of about 7 lakhs, that proper floor protection arrangements had been made, and that the Gazipur drain had already been constructed and its capacity was over 5,000 cubic feet per second, whereas the discharge from the resettlement colonies of Khichripur and Trilokpuri was estimated to be only 600 to 800 cubic feet per second. Again, in the Coordination Committee meeting of 10 June 1976, Sushil Kumar, Chief Secretary, stated after discussion with, Chief Engineer, Floods, Delhi Administration, that the

Lies, Half-Truths and Convenient Conscience

inlets in Ghazipur drain were not needed because the water itself was likely to go in the drain by gravity. In spite of these hard facts, propaganda about the alleged low level of resettlement colonies was carried out with impunity. There have been heavy rains in Delhi during the monsoon of 1976-77. The arrangement of Trilokpuri-Khichripur complex proved totally effective and there was no accumulation of water at any point, while the old and so-called well-developed areas, including the Ring Road, were flooded. In fact, during the worst Delhi flood of 1977, only one resettlement colony, Jahangirpuri, out of the 27 resettlement colonies developed during the emergency, was flooded, and that, too, due to non-completion of the drainage work which had been taken in hand but not attended to seriously after I relinquished charge in April 1977.

The press had its own share of convenient conscience. For instance, this is what *Blitz*, which is now talking of the black deeds of "clearances" of the emergency, published on 3 April 1976 after its Special Correspondent visited the Trilokpuri complex:

> Never has so much been achieved in such a short time. This, more or less, sums up the stupendous feat of providing 70,000 squatter families, living in small, dingy, unhygienic hovels scattered all over the capital, permanent housing sites in well developed colonies in less than eight months. . . .
>
> Six months ago, Khichripur and Patparganj were small, sleepy villages across the river. Hundreds of acres of land there was lying barren, though notified by the DDA and kept for future use. But where the *Blitz* visited the area last week, it was bustling with activity. . . the entire Trilokpuri colony was studded with poles fitted with tube lights. Thus, the basic necessities like electricity, water and other public conveniences are available well before the fresh batches of Jhuggi families arrive. . . .
>
> Simple, easy-to-follow lay-out plans were available at the D.D.A.'s office on the site and the engineering staff was posted there to provide on the spot know-how. Besides, sample houses in all three phases have been built for the people to have an idea of the type of construction they have to go in for. . . .

I am reminded of a story. Before independence, a Rai Sahib used to praise the British Government. After independence, he started praising the new government. Someone asked Rai Sahib as to how he had suddenly changed, "I have not changed, it is the government which has changed," replied Rai Sahib.

CHAPTER VII

THE DISEASE THAT AFFLICTS US ALL

> O my rivals, let's stop all this.
> This nastiness and flattery.
> Let's think about our fate,
> About the disease that afflicts us all.
>
> YEVTUSHENKO

By the very nature of the job I handled for about six and a half years as Vice Chairman, Delhi Development Authority, I came in clash with powerful vested interests—land racketeers, speculators, and those who tried to build bases of political and financial power at the cost of the planned development of the city. It is these people who are now engineering all types of false, frivolous and motivated complaints. Some officers, affected by jealousy, are playing their own part. For such persons, the current atmosphere of hostility has come as a God-sent opportunity.

HOSTILE NETWORK

I could never imagine that a hostile network would be woven around me merely on the suspicion that the alleged power structure operating in Delhi had drawn within its orbit the activities of the Delhi Development Authority, and that no one would care to ask the obvious questions: which are the programmes and policies implemented during the emergency that had not been implemented before the emergency? Were not the procedures and practices adopted exactly the same as in the earlier period?

Clearly, I had not taken into account the subtle and clever role which the vested interests could play. With top persons annoyed or kept in dark, the manipulators, the racketeers, the rival bureaucrats and the personal enemies could not ask for better opportunity to wreak vengeance. For them, the time had come for the "kill." Now or never seemed to be their motto.

Through the so-called labour leaders and other hostile interests whose land-racketeering and nefarious activities had been checked by me firmly and fearlessly, notwithstanding the *siapas* and demonstrations staged at my residence even at night, a number of cases were referred to the Central Bureau of Investigation which, however, could find nothing. In reply to a question in Parliament, the Minister of Works and Housing, Sikander Bakht, stated on 12 July 1977, that the allegations against me were found to be baseless.

The vested interests could hardly swallow this. For them, the defeat had come too early. They were at a loss to save their face. They, therefore, pulled the wires and forced the authorities to dish out something. A vicious propaganda was set in motion. Old cases—some as old as ten to fifteen years—were dug out. The Minister who had spoken the plain truth was criticized. The ears of persons in authority were poisoned. "Cassius-like" conspiracies were hatched, and lack of charges against me was described as victory for the alleged power structure functioning in Delhi during the emergency.

When a local Member of Parliament, Vijay Kumar Malhotra, reportedly tried to vouchsafe for my integrity and hard work, a false story about my relationship with him was coined and circulated notwithstanding the public denials by Malhotra himself, and the statement of the Chief Executive Councillor Kedar Nath Sahani in the Metropolitan Council. The truth is that not only I am not related to Malhotra but also that I had not seen his face till he became the Chief Executive Councillor of Delhi. His opinion about me, I am sure, is based upon my conduct and performance during his tenure (1967-71) as Chief Executive Councillor.

On 25 May 1977, the Union Home Ministry issued a notification appointing a Fact Finding Committee to collect facts about "the programmes for slum clearance, removal of encroachments, demolition, beautification, etc." It comprised two members—R.C. Jain and D.K. Aggarwal. The choice of R.C. Jain, who was to act as the senior member of the Committee, came as a rude shock to me. There could be no worse personal enemy of mine than Jain. This had been amply demonstrated during his tenure (1972-74) as Special Assistant to the then Lieutenant Governor. Many others who had known his performance raised their eyebrows, but they preferred to keep quiet. Such skin-deep is our commitment to the concept of justice.

In my written statement to the Commission, this is what I stated:

> Jain was known to Shri Baleshwar Prasad. Soon after the latter took over as Lt. Governor in early 1972, Jain was appointed as his Special Assistant. His appointment was beginning of all sorts of troubles for me. He started concentrating powers in his hands—not for the sake of delivering the goods, but for the sake of power itself.
>
> Jain had a special eye on the Delhi Development Authority. Both he and Baleshwar Prasad had developed a weakness for residential plots. They did not show much respect for the superior claims of others. When I tried to explain the correct position, Jain poisoned the mind of Baleshwar Prasad. He was given the impression that I was a stumbling block. Since I could not be got rid of, my appointment being in the hands of Cabinet Comittee, Jain thought of a device to cut me off. He got appointed his close friend and batch-mate, V. Shankaran, as Commissioner in the Delhi Development Authority, and started dealing with him direct, eliminating me in the process.

Today the Commission is looking into the allegations in respect of violation of "well-established conventions, administrative procedures and practices." Is it justified that the person chosen to collect—rather "obtain"—material against the alleged defaulters was himself guilty of flagrantly violated the "well-established conventions, administrative procedures and practices"?

My relationship with Jain was further embittered by what came to be known as the VIP Land Grab Scandal which came before the Supreme Court in Writ Petition No. 340-1972 (original jurisdiction).

The story of the VIP Land Grab Scandal, in brief, was that

in collaboration with certain members of the nominated Managing Committee of the New Friends Co-operative Housing Society, the Lieutenant Governor and his Special Assistant, Jain, removed some old members/allottees of the plots in the society and got enrolled in their places what came to be known as VIP members. These included Baleshwar Prasad's nephew, S.V. Purushottam, whose address was given care of K.K. Sirivastava, Chief Secretary, Delhi Administration, and R.C. Jain's wife, Mrs Mohini Jain, whose address was not given care of her husband but as Banaras Art House. There was an obvious attempt to hide the identity.

Everything was done in what the Supreme Court described, in its order dated 4 April 1975, as "undue haste." The Chief Justice observed: "Undue haste in rushing through the allotment procedure and the list of new allottees speak for themselves." A letter was obtained from the President of the Managing Committee of the Society on 26 January 1974 (Republic Day) and replied on the same day by the Lieutenant Governor, giving approval to the deletion of the old members and enrolment of the new ones (VIP) including his nephew and Mrs R.C. Jain.

Jain knew that I would never be a party to such an act. So he manoeuvred to keep me out. Apparently, he persuaded the Lieutenant Governor not to show the case or file to me. He also knew that it would be difficult for the Lieutenant Governor to over-rule me on the file.

To look into the manipulation and deletion of old members and enrolment of new ones, the Supreme Court appointed Justice Debabrata Mukerjee, a retired judge of the Calcutta High Court, as Chairman. Mukerjee held that the deletion of the old members and enrolment of new ones was illegal. The findings of Mukerjee were confirmed by the Supreme Court. In its judgement (W.P. No. 340 of 1972, and No. 1526 of 1972 and No. 286 of 1974), the Supreme Court made, inter alia, the following observations:

> The Chairman [Justice Debabrata Mukerjee] declared that of the 60 new members who had been described as very important persons 21 did not have applications for membership and 38 were not legally admitted members and could not be

included in the list. The Chairman said that the *allotment of plots in their favour could not be upheld.*

In view of the importance of issue involved and the gravity of the situation where interest of ordinary citizens was sacrificed to meet the interest of *persons of importance and influence* this Court took the aforesaid steps in order to put an end to the litigation and the controversies. . . .

The Chairman noticed that "many of these 60 persons were high placed Government officials and friends and relations of persons prominent in public life."

Thus, the fact of manipulation was clearly established. It is immaterial whether a particular person was technically held guilty or not. In fact, this was not the issue before the court.

Parliamentary proceedings for the period April-May 1974 are revealing. Chandra Shekhar, A.B. Vajpayee and other senior members of Parliament vehemently criticized the enrolment of the VIP members. Jyotirmoy Basu, MP, disclosed that R.C. Jain had met senior officers and VIPs and obtained their signatures on the application forms for membership of the society and allotment of land.

The extreme hostility and bias of R.C. Jain were evident from the manner in which he proceeded after the appointment of the Fact Finding Committee. An impression was created in a subtle way that the officers of the Central Bureau of Investigation had been put on the track of DDA officials. The attempt was to overawe the junior officers, create a fear psychosis and obtain incriminating statements against me. They were made to believe that slums and squatters clearance was some sort of a criminal action from which they could escape by blaming me for decision as well as for implementation. They could blame me not only for what I had ordered or approved but also for their own omissions and procedural lapses. To escape, or even to get rewarded, the only qualification prescribed was to point out an accusing finger against me.

The bias of R.C. Jain was also evident from the suppression or underplaying of material facts, including the unanimous agreement of the leading political parties, the old cabinet decisions in respect of squatters and slum clearance and Land Acquisition Schemes, and well-established practice of deploying demolition squad and taking over of possession of land by the Land Acquisition Collector. There are a number of other instances to support my contention. A distorted picture was sought to be placed before the Commission.

As soon as Jain's Committee was announced, I met Sikander Bakht, and apprised him briefly of Jain's animus against me. The Minister told me that he had not been consulted, and he did not know who Jain was. He, however, promised to look into the matter. I left the matter at that. Then, suddenly a statement of Home Minister in the end of July 1977 appeared in the press, indicating that the government might take action on the report of the Fact Finding Committee. Knowing Jain's hostility, this alarmed me. I put in a written protest to Secretary, Ministry of Works and Housing, on 2 August 1977, stating that I had reasonable grounds to apprehend that I would not get fair, impartial and objective treatment at the hands of Fact Finding Committee, the senior member of which was Jain. In this protest, which was immediately transmitted by the Ministry of Works and Housing to the Home Ministry, I had, inter alia, stated:

> When Jain was working as Special Assistant to the Lt. Governor/Chairman, Delhi Development Authority, I was the Vice Chairman. Unfortunately, the relationship between myself and Jain became strained due to various reasons. This fact is known to the various officers of the Delhi Administration and the Delhi Development Authority.
>
> Although the Committee has been named as Fact Finding Committee, yet it is clear that in the collection, selection and presentation of facts conscious or unconscious bias creeps in.

What reply did I get? On 5 August 1977, a press note was issued by the Central Bureau of Investigation, apparently at the instance of links which Jain had in the Home Ministry, stating that a case had been registered for investigation against me for allegedly approving in 1974 increased rate for engagement of trucks—ignoring, of course, the vital facts that recommendation to this effect had been made to me by the senior officers of the department, that the actual cost of the trucks had gone up manifold, that the repeated efforts by the officers of the department to engage trucks at the lower rate had failed, that clearance operations had to be postponed on a number of occasions, thereby causing inconvenience to public and loss to public exchequer, that tenders obtained twice through the press advertisements confirmed the justification of the increased rate, and that payment had been made over the years through the Finance and Accounts Branch of the DDA. The attempt to defame, browbeat and pressurize me was too crude to go unnoticed.

The procedure adopted in calling and examining of witnesses was equally astounding, and should shock the conscience of any respecter of law and justice. The junior officers were called in a closed room in which sat the two senior officers, Jain and Aggarwal, about whom it had been made known that any slight hint from them could throw the officers out of job and involve them in some trouble or the other. The impression was sufficient in most cases to obtain whatever statements were required and to fix evidence in support of pre-determined conclusions.

There were other aspects of the hostile network spread by Jain which need to be delineated. Evidence was sought to be noted in the most extraordinary manner. For instance, after the statement of R.M. Vats, the then Commissioner, DDA, had been formally recorded by the Fact Finding Committee, he was lured to make an off-the-cuff remark over a cup of tea. He is supposed to have said that at my instance he went to the Prime Minister's house during the period of my visit to Vancouvre (Canada) to attend the United Nations Conference on HABITAT in May 1976. Words were put in his mouth to say that he saw me, Tamta, Bhinder, Alawadi and others visiting the Prime Minister's house regularly, and that I had instructed him to take the files and papers to discuss the cases in the Prime Minister's house. Casual remarks, supposedly made, were reduced to writing subsequently by Jain and sent to Vats in the form of a letter for confirmation. Vats was in a fix. If he denied, he would incur the displeasure of Jain and his links or associates in the power structure; if he did not, he would feel the prick of conscience and would also have to explain which files and records he had taken to the Prime Minister's house. He chose the middle path. He denied the material portion but remained silent over my suggestion to visit the Prime Minister's house, in my absence, to attend to the visitors who came there practically every morning in connection with representations and grievances concerning various departments, including the DDA.

The incident is significant not for what Vats said or did not say, but for the manner in which incriminating statements were sought to be obtained and witnesses later on confronted with such statements before the Commision.

S.C. Dixit, Deputy Commissioner (Implementation), had experience similar to Vats'. My successor advised Dixit to coordinate the correspondence of various branches of the DDA with the Fact Finding Committee. Dixit had nothing to do with the clearance of Turkman Gate area or any other clearance. One day he was asked by Jain to discuss the progress of the correspondence. After discussion, Jain vaguely spoke about the Turkman Gate incident. Being not conversant with the background and facts of the case, Dixit gave a casual reply. To his great surprise, Dixit, after a day or so, received a letter from Jain, stating that during our discussions you informed the Committee that force was used in demolishing houses and that this information was being placed on record. A bewildered Dixit had no other option but to reply that he was not concerned with the Turkman Gate case and was, therefore, not in a position to say whether force was used or not. What happened subsequently need not be discussed here. My purpose is only to indicate how certain statements were sought to be extracted and placed on record.

Jain reportedly returned the notes and letters, sent by some branches of the DDA, which explained the correct position. Instead, he confined himself to the oral statements, extracted from junior officers in a closed room. It did not matter to him if such oral statements were at variance with the written records or minutes of the meeting. For instance, a junior officer was made to say that there were elements of surprise in the organization of clearance operations, although the written records would show that survey of squatters was generally conducted beforehand and the squatters' families given clearance/alltoment slips in advance. Hardly anyone complained about the element of surprise. Moreover, after June 1976, all decisions in respect of clearance were taken by a Coordination Committee comprising senior officers of various departments and organizations specially set up for the purpose. How could there be any element of surprise when clearance operations were being carried out practically every day, and the operation in a particular area was usually spread over a number of days.

Jain also conveniently forgot that the procedures followed in regard to the clearance and resettlement of squatters were the same as in vogue during the period Jain himself had been working as Special Assistant to the Lieutenant Governor. If there was anything legally or administratively wrong in the procedure, why did he not get it corrected? It is ironical that those officers, who had themselves been party to certain procedures and practices, are today, without any compunction of conscience, denouncing them as something illegal and irregular, deserving punishment. D.K. Aggarwal, the second member of the Fact Finding Committee, who was working as Superintendent of Police (Central) in 1968, himself took ten companies of the Police Force, including Delhi Armed Police, to remove the squatters from the Kela Godown, near Qutab Road, and New Delhi Railway Station. If that was not considered intimidatory, why deployment of small additional force for the clearance work should now be condemned as intimidatory and illegal?

After obtaining statements from the officers to fit in their predetermined framework, the Committee asked me on phone in mid-August to appear before it. No precise indication was given about the cases in respect of which the Committee wished to examine me.

Taken by Surprise

I had asked the Fact Finding Committee to examine me in question and answer form. Knowing the disposition of Jain, I suspected that I would not be examined on material points, so that I could be taken by surprise before the Commission, and should not be able to refer to the official records to prove that whatever was done was in accordance with the government policy and programme. But my request was not heeded. My statement was recorded on rather general issues and none of the specific cases, the so-called case studies (five cases) with which I was suddenly confronted before the Commission, was put to me. This was done in spite of my written request to the Committee that if it wanted to include any specific case relating to me or the

DDA in its report it should examine me with regard to that case.

There is yet another aspect of the hostile network. There was implicit inducement as well as threat. If the witness stated that everything done during the emergency in the sphere of Delhi's development was a "black" deed and was done under fear and coercion from above, he was not troubled. If, on the other hand, the witness stated that what was done was in accordance with past policy and practice, he was mercilessly harassed.

When the Committee questioned me about the orders allegedly issued from the Prime Minister's house, I told them whatever I had to say in this regard would be stated before the Shah Commission. At the same time, I made it clear that in regard to clearance and resettlement of squatters and slum-dwellers, policy decision of the government and competent authorities already existed and the question of obtaining orders from anyone did not arise.

This was obviously not to the liking of powers that be. Soon after I gave the above indications, orders suspending me from service were passed. The attempt to pressurize, harass and break me was revolting. About eight months have passed and no charge-sheet has been served on me. In an organization which has to deal with highly controversial and inconvenient matters and in which various interests operate behind the scene, all sorts of papers and files are being picked up and subjected to most unsympathetic scrutiny with a view to finding some fault or the other. Even the provision of the vigilance manual of the central government, advising that officer should not be suspended if the purpose can be served by leave or transfer, has been ignored. I was already on foreign service to the Institute of Urban Affairs, and had nothing to do with the DDA. B.R. Tamta, on the other hand, was not suspended, presumably because he toed the indicated line. There are, I understand, over hundred officers in Delhi against whom reports for investigation were launched, but none of them was suspended.

From a National Hero to a "National Villain"

What is still more painful is that no regard whatsoever was shown to my outstanding record of service and unquestioned integrity which had been forcefully certified by such eminent senior civil servants as Bhagwan Sahay, Dharma Vira, A.D. Pandit, Dr J.N. Khosla, and late Dr A.N. Jha.

No consideration was given to the fact that as far back as 1971 I was awarded Padma Shri for, what my citation described, "pioneering work" in the field of urban development. Padma Bhushan was conferred on me in 1977. No significance was attached to the publication of my book and a number of articles in leading newspapers and magazines, and other contributions made by me to the literature on human settlement, urbanization, housing and slum clearance, etc.

Overnight from a national hero—winner of Padma Shri and Padma Bhushan—I was made a "national villain." My fault was that I happened to occupy a particular post at a particular time, and was not prepared to step out of my island of truth and pose like a traitor and self-condemned criminal, throw mud on others, and hypocritically comdemn a programme and policy which had been formulated with the concurrence of leading political parties and the implementation of which was totally in public interest. Subtle hints were given to me that I should become a sort of "approver" and pass on the "blame" to others. I marvelled at the lack of morality and the ignorance of the persons who gave such suggestions. Was clearance of some of the most inhuman slum or allotment of 1,000 hectares of developed land with market value of about Rs 200 crores, or disbursement of about Rs 9 crores of loan at only 4 per cent rate of interest, or creation of stable and development-oriented avenues of employment, preservation of historical legacy, or general environmental upgardation of the city, an "excess" for which one should feel ashamed?

Perversion of values and dominance of superficial thinking is, indeed, appalling.

> Superficiality—worse than being blind
> You can see but not want to.
> Are you ignorant, you?
> Or may be it is from fear of ripping up roots
> Of sheltering trees, leaving not a trace,
> Not so much as a stick planted in their place.
> We hurry along with half an answer,
> Bearing our shallowness like a treasure.
> No, no, not in cold calculation

But in an instinct of self-preservation.
Then comes the snuffing out.
The inability to flee or flight
And the feathers of our tamed wings
Become nasty pillows for the night.

HALF AN ANSWER

Were we not hurrying along with half an answer? This question began to haunt me as soon as the proceedings of the Commission —"assistance stage" as it was called—commenced. Witnesses after witnesses were produced to make all sorts of statements, mostly tutored and unsupported by any authentic document, to outline a pre-conceived pattern. The damage caused by the prejudicial approach of the Fact Finding Committee could be clearly perceived.

In what manner, I began to wonder, the Commission wanted my assistance? Doubts began to disturb me. I began to nurse the uncomfortable feeling that the procedure adopted virtually amounted to securing my assistance to clip my own wings. Out of the thousands of cases with which I had to deal with, I was suddenly confronted with the details of the five or six cases which were more than two or three years old and in respect of which I had no forewarning. I helplessly watched the witnesses who appeared to have been reared on promises, or whose instinct of self-preservation had been successfully exploited. Nor was it clear to me why it was necessary to mount a hostile publicity campaign. Was the intention to demoralize or frighten? And what about my right to cross-examination? Had it not been rendered ineffective? Some of these doubts, I thought, I should bring to the notice of the Commission. This is what I pleaded:

> When the witnesses appeared before the Commission at the "assistance stage" of Inquiry, they had already been pinned down by the Fact Finding Committee and committed to a particular statement. I did not have the opportunity to cross-examine the witnesses at the earliest opportunity. On the other hand, I was asked to make a statement on oath, and subjected to cross-examination in respect of the cases and matters about which no previous detailed intimation had been given to me.

Consequently, my defence has already become known, and the right to cross-examination, which is now being given to me, has been rendered ineffective. The witnesses would now reply in the light of information they have gained from my statement and my replies to the cross-examination. This amounts to virtual denial of right to cross-examination, and is against the rules of natural justice. This aspect of the enquiry proceedings is particularly relevant in my case because the very nature of my duties was such that I happened to annoy a number of powerful vested interests and they are now making every efforts to settle old scores. . . .Circulation of rumours, biased press reports and publication of carelessly written books have vitiated the general atmosphere.

Terms of Reference

In the heat of the moment, the terms of reference of the Commission also seemed to have been relegated. In my statement, I invited the attention of the Commission to this aspect. I stated:

The terms of reference of the Commission include inquiry into the allegations of "indiscriminate and high-handed demolition of houses, huts, shops, buildings, structures and destructions of property in the name of slum clearance or enforcement of town planning or land use schemes in the cities and towns resulting, inter alia, in a large number of people becoming homeless or having to move far away from the places of their vocation."

I submit that nothing has been done in the name of slum clearance. All the actions taken are covered by the approved schemes, policies and programme of the central government and the Delhi Development Authority. I merely got implemented these approved schemes and policies. Neither the central government nor the DDA expressed any doubt that any of my action was not covered by the approved and well-established pattern and policies

The policies and programmes as well as the manner of their implementation were the same as in vogue before the promulgation of emergency. In respect of buildings to be cleared under the Slum Clearance Act and in respect of the

Land Acquisition Schemes, the policy decisions had been taken by the central government and the competent authorities much before the promulgation of emergency. No fresh policy decision was taken.

The speed of work, however, increased, primarily because the pressure of vested interests abated, the government and the DDA remained firm, and the squatters and slum-dwellers cooperated with the authorities as they got convinced that everybody was being treated alike and the resettlement at regular sites would be in the their overall interest. Nothing has been done under any guise or in the name of slum clearance scheme. Terms of reference imply consideration of only those cases by the Commission in which action has been taken under guise or in the name of slum clearance scheme, and not in accordance with the prevailing schemes and procedures.

As a sequel to the implementation of approved schemes no one was rendered homeless. Everybody was provided with alternative accommodation which was invariably better, both in terms of space and environment, than the previous site which had been unauthorizedly occupied or illegally constructed. Nor were employment avenues, as demonstrated in earlier chapter, adversely affected. In this context, do the terms of reference of the Commission really permit consideration of the so-called "demolition cases" of the DDA?

MISGIVINGS ABOUT PROCEDURES

In respect of some vital procedural aspects, too, I had serious misgivings. I thought that rules of natural justice had not been respected. I stated:

> Immediately after the appointment of the Commission, vide Ministry of Home Affairs' notification No. S.O. 374 (E), dated the 28th May, 1977, the Commission issued a notification in pursuance of clause (b) of sub-rule (2) of rule 5 of the Commission of Inquiry (Central) Rules, 2972. In this notification, it was stipulated: "Members of the public are requested to

file the complaints or statements regarding the matters specified above either individually or collectively within a period of one month from the date of publication of this notification."

It is clear from the above that the statements/complaints about matters specified in the said notification had to be submitted to the Commission within one month. A number of complaints have been received after the stipulated date. Some of the complaints were entertained on the date of hearing itself or a few days before it. In view of the stipulation quoted above, these complaints may be excluded from the purview of consideration of the Commission.

Under Section 5(A) of the Commission of Inquiry Act, the Commission is empowered to utilize the services of certain officers and investigating agencies for conducting investigation pertaining to inquiry. Such officers and investigation agencies have to be officers of the Commission or appointed under its directions. In the demolition cases, the statements were recorded and investigations carried out, not by the officers of the Commission or under its directions, but by a Committee, known as Fact Finding Committee, which was appointed by the Ministry of Home Affairs vide its notification No. U-11-11/5/77. dated 25 May 1977. Use by the Commission of any material collected by the committee is, therefore, not covered by the provisions of Commissions of Inquiry Act. All the case summaries were prepared on the basis of the material collected by the Committee. This is not legally permissible.

The Fact Finding Committee was appointed without any authority of law. The Committee "pinned down" the witnesses. It even got statement signed from them. Even when some statements were re- recorded by the Commission, the witnesses, particularly government officials, could not but repeat what the Committee had extracted or obtained from them in a closed room. They had been "committed" to a particular statement, and could not deviate from it for fear of unfavourable consequences. This, I believe, is against the rules of natural justice, and has seriously prejudiced my defence.

New Heroes

What happened after the emergency? New "heroes" came on the scene. These heroes were committed, not to the planned development, but to the planned destruction of the city. Under the cloak of endless talk of "emergency excesses" they hid their own excesses against the poor and helpless cities. They confused the public and the authorities. The landscape was ravaged. Posterity was burdened with an albatross around its neck. This is what *Hindustan Times* wrote on 12 November 1977:

> Hundreds of people have put up shanties in West Delhi with impunity. The manner in which unauthorised shops have re-appeared in Tilak Nagar is totally shocking. Similarly, large-scale unauthorised encroachment on public land in the trans-Yamuna colonies during the past six months has gone unchecked but not unnoticed.... One can see unauthorised bazars coming up in areas like Karol Bagh, Sadar Bazar, Chandni Chowk and Kashmere Gate....
>
> Apart from unauthorised encroachments on pavements and on public land, hundreds and thousands of people have started building houses in different parts of the city without bothering to get the construction plans sanctioned from either the Corporation or the DDA. The stock reply from the police, the DMC or the DDA is "We don't want to repeat emergency excesses."

The *Statesman* (28 September 1977) contained the following comments on the subject:

> Never before has "unauthorised construction", an euphemism for encroachment on public land, enjoyed such a boom as at present. Word has spread that the janta stealing the janta's land will be immune....

The same newspaper quoted S.N. Bansal, Chairman of the Standing Committee of the Corporation:

> People start construction on a Saturday morning, mostly on

a second Saturday, which is a Government holiday and comlete nearly 75% of the construction by Monday morning....

By the time our demolition squad reaches the spot, the party greets us with a stay order from the courts. Some times a hostile crowd is also there, ready to attack the demolition squad....

The above press comments clearly show that what was done during the emergency was in public interest; otherwise why should re-emergence of encroachments and illegal construction be condemned so earnestly. Incidently, these comments also show how the vested interests manipulate, and it was this manipulation that was intended to be curbed firmly during the emergency.

New demolitions are again being carried out. Appendix I gives particulars of these demolitions. It will be noticed that from the end of September 1977 to March 1978 6,269 demolitions have been carried out by the DDA alone. The old policy and procedures which are sought to be condemned before the Commission are being followed, except that alternative accomodation is not being provided even to the jhuggi-dwellers. This approach, unfortunately, ignores the considerations elaborated in Chapter II and does not take into account the normal inflow of the poor migrants to a metropolitan city. The current approach needs to be modified. The new migrants, as argued earlier, must be diverted to the "resettlement/migrant" colonies, where the sites could be allotted to them on rent. Planned and purposive settlement of the urban poor is the crying need of the current times. It was answered during the period of emergency, and the backlogs were also cleared.

In view of what was done before the emergency and what is being done after, it will be unfair to allege that something wrong was done during the emergency or any excess was committed.

REAL JUSTICE

As regards the speed of work, it undoubtedly increased. There were valid reasons for it. Even otherwise, was it wrong to shake off lethargy, eliminate "gossip cafes" from our offices, relieve the tyranny of Kafkasque world of papers, full of sound and furry, signifying nothing? Is it not correct that the speed attained during the emergency should be normal if we have to extricate ourselves from the vicious grip of poverty and underdevelopment? Was it not courageous to keep the obstructionists and obscurantists at bay and thus serve the cause of real truth, real justice and real humanism? Can we be really free if the gap between our productivity and that of developed world goes on widening?

There are two courses open for dealing with the slum and squatters population. One is to assert the lawful authority, that is to issue notices, say of twenty-four hours, and throw the families out, there being no legal obligation to provide alternative accomodation. The other course is to talk to the slum-dwellers and squatters, and persuade them to shift by making available alternative accommodation on regular basis—taking care, of course, to ensure that political and financial vested interests do not intervene. Which of the two courses is just, human and workable? Will the cause of real justice, real humanism be served by asserting the lawful authority in a technical manner? "Notices" have relevance only for those who are in a position to make alternative arrangements on their own and whose level of social and educational development does not permit exploitation by vested interests.

Do we want semblance or reality of justice. No law can answer the needs of absolute justice. In a country like ours, where social sense is not developed and where the administration is beset with routine, the gap between law and justice tends to become too wide and the community is held to ransom by those who know how to exploit the technicality of law. This is particularly true in the sphere of metropolitan planning where social and environmental costs of delays are extremely high.

In this connection, I am reminded of a case in which an unauthorized stone-crusher and about half a dozen squatters of magazine road held up the completion of an important road designed to provide a direct link from the Wazirabad Barrage to the ring road The main objective of this link was to remove a traffic hazard by preventing heavy vehicles to enter the residential colony of Timarpur. The link should have been completed immediately after the completion of Wazirabad Barrage. But the "stay order" from the court and the propensity of the operator to exploit the technicalities of law held up the project. In the meanwhile, two young sons of a police officer going on a motorcycle were knocked down by a truck from the Wazirabad Barrage. Both of them died. Justice was done to them! How many such "justices" were done during the four long years for which the project was delayed. How much the community suffered in social and environmental cost? Neither those who sit in their ivory tower and use their intellect in the service of technicalities nor those who seek political advantage even at heavy social costs ponder over their actions.

In this context, it is pertinent to ask: who has really committed excesses? Is it really not those who drew fat salaries and spent their time in playing "game of words," who kept important development schemes pending for 30 or 40 years, who administered technical rather than real justice, and who allowed poor people to languish in extremely unhealthy localities?

Administrative Ethos

Routine and casual character of our administrative set-up is notorious. As far back as 1905, Lord Curzon, in his famous farewell speech at the Byculla Club, Bombay, described the Indian bureaucracy as "the most mechanised and lifeless of all form of administration." Notwithstanding the fact that more than 70 years have elapsed when the above remarks were made, the "lifeless" character of our administration has not basically changed; in fact, it has taken a sharper turn towards ineffectiveness. Explanation for this is to be found in our national ethos, in our values, in our tendency to keep a wide gap between what we preach and what we practise.

Every day, we hear journalists, intellectuals, politicians and senior civil servants denouncing the old-fashioned methods and stressing the needs for result-oriented administration. But what happens in actual practice? Whenever anyone tries to break the shackles of routine and impart dynamism, he finds himself in trouble. His firmness is described as ruthlessness, his commitment as personal ambition, and his speed as rashness. And he is soon shown the way out. On the other hand, those who spend their life-time in tying red tapes over the blue flaps of bludgeoning files have smooth sailing. Let me give an example.

In Delhi, large tracts of lands are owned by various departments and ministries of the central government. These lands were under the charge of senior officers of the rank of Joint Secretary or Commissioner, and sizeable staff was engaged for their management. But they were allowed to be illegally occupied by shopkeepers, mechanics, wood merchants, ware houses, etc. Except for pushing papers up and down and holding scores of meeting, no steps were taken for over two decades to retrieve these lands. Consequently, public lands worth crores remained in the hands of racketeers. Cityscape was uglified. Traffic jams and accidents increased, and execution of development projects inordinately delayed. After years of deliberation, the central government recognized that the DDA was the only agency that could solve the problem and transferred all these lands to it in 1975. By discarding ineffective methods and taking a courageous stand against vested interests, the DDA solved the problem in about a year. The skyline improved. Traffic hazards were reduced and long-pending development projects were executed.

What were the results? What happened to those who took their jobs seriously? Those who tried to be result-oriented, and spent long hours in the field under scorching sun, taking quick decisions and settling cases at the spot, instead of pushing papers in airconditioned offices, find themselves in the dock and are subjected to ridicule on behalf of those who showed nothing but contempt for law and morality. On the other hand, those who considered themselves too refind and sophisticated to soil their hands in the mire of slums, squatters and illegal constructions are leading a comfortable life.

INTIMIDATION

The hostile element did not relent even when the matter came up before the Commission. When I started defending the action taken, some persons, who had obviously come with a purpose, started heckling me. When they found that this technique did not work, they even staged a demonstration in the premises of the Commission on 21 December 1977. I had to seek the protection of the Commission. My application of 22 December 1977 to the Commission read as under:

In respone to the letter of the Commission, I have been attending its proceedings in order to render whatever assistance I can. Unfortunately, for the last two days, the atmosphere has been vitiated by certain persons. Notwithstanding the fact that against 120 houses cleared about 1,000 (200 flats, 600 residential plots and 200 industrial and commercial plots) alternative allotments were made, a communal colour is sought to be given to the implementation of what was purely a slum clearance scheme after liberalising the Corporation Resolution which denied alternative accomodation to the "unauthorised occupants." Some persons made concocted, defamatory and reckless statements, such as those pertaining to the "second Pakistan" and myself and other persons overseeing the demolition/clearance work. All types of remarks were also made when these proceedings were going on, and in the evening a hostile and aggressive demonstraction was also staged within the premises of the Commission to overawe, demoralise and intimidate me. . . I seek protection of the Commission and request it to take such other suitable action as it may consider appropriate in the matter.

It is an unfortunate aspect of our public life that while those who think that a lot of good work has been done sit quietly at home and confine themselves to lip sympathy, the hostile elements, taking advantage of the peculiar atmosphere, conspire in every possible way to impute motives, twist facts, and denigrate the man who gave the best part of his life to Delhi's development without taking even a day's rest. It appears that:

The best lack all convictions, while the worst
Are full of passionate intensity.

PUBLICITY

The manner in which the Commission proceedings were publicized showed that those very techniques, which were intended to be denounced, were actually the guiding stars. Some aspects were magnified, some underplayed, some slanted, some suppressed, and some, as V.C. Shukla pointed out in his complaint to the Commission, "manufactured." For researchers of modern media system, it will be a good exercise to examine how certain statements and observations were ignored, while others, which had no relevance to the evidence on the file or point at issue, got the maximum publicity. Was the intention to defame and denigrate or find out the truth and serve the cause of justice?

For instance, there was no evidence on the file about the so-called involvement of "Youth Congress" in the proposed construction of commercial complex in Turkman Gate area. Only public objections had been invited by the DDA, with the approval of the central government, in regard to the proposed change of land-use, as had been done in several other cases in the past. Morever, the DDA has never sold any commercial space except through public auction. How could then the question of favouring anyone ar se? During the emergency, the DDA sold a number of developed "tower plots" worth Rs 2 or 3 crores each, in the prestigious commercial complex of Nehru Place. If any individual or group had to be favoured, why could not one or two such "tower plots" be made available to the "individual" or the "group" straightway? What was the necessity of waiting for an uncertain proposal in distant future? Notwithstanding all these facts, wide publicity was given to the "money-spinning project," "Youth Congress's interest," and "political battle" in which the DDA got involved. (For keeping the records straight, I have given in Appendix III extracts from my statement to the Commission in respect of five specific cases.)

OFFICERS' PREDICAMENT

The extreme difficulty in which the officers found themselves is best illustrated by what Ranbir Singh, an executive officer of the DDA, who was previously a revenue officer of Haryana, stated almost involuntarily before the Commission on 7 April 1978. He said something like this:

> I was a revenue officer from Haryana on deputation to the DDA. Due to hostile attitude of Bansi Lal, the then Chief Minister of Haryana, I was forced to resign. For the purpose of pension, I lost 19 years of service. Now, I am being victimized merely because I carried out the approved policy of the

government and the DDA in the same manner as was being done before the emergency.

The Fact Finding Committee was totally prejudiced. It deliberately suppressed material facts. Why did it pick up either the Vice-Chairman or the executive officers? What about several inter-mediary officers? Why did the Committee ignore the written records, such as the registers of surveys, allotment slips, the minutes of various meetings, past precedents, demolition duty-rosters, police *roznamcha* reports, etc?

How can I defend myself against the state apparatus? I had made a request for legal assistance. But the same was refused. On the other hand, both the government and Commission are assisted by highly paid counsels (P.N. Lekhi is getting about Rs 900 per day and Karl Khandawala Rs 1600 per day, besides other remunerations for advice, discussions, etc.) In these circumstances, can there be an equal legal fight, a fair and just exposition of the entire case? I do not think there is any precedent anywhere where a public servant who has discharged his duties in accordance with the old policies and practices had been put in the dock and subjected to all type of questioning without getting any support from the government or from any other source.

Against the tutored witnesses, who made earlier depositions without caring to show any sanctioned building plan or any written documents in support of their legal ownership, I can hardly do anything. The Commission may send its own officials to see that the structures, which were not vacated voluntarily, are still standing. Only those who were willing to shift by securing alternative allotment actually moved; otherwise how could so many structures be still standing in those very localities. You doubt our version about the voluntarily movement. We know the truth—we who daily meet the people. In those days, conditions were different. Now, if you ask any one to stand in queue at the bus stand, he will slap you. In those days if you suggested to the unauthorized builder or encroacher to remove his shack or structure by simultaneously offering him an alternative site or house, he thanked.

Ranbir Singh said all this with a lump in his throat. The statement came from the heart rather than the head, and was true expression of a bewildered, pained and tortured mind. I had myself often wondered whether there was really any other way of tearing the wall of hostility and conflict except by striking my head against it.

AN EPISODE

After the proceedings of Commission, on 7 April 1978, some young men whom I had seem practically every day in the Commission room engaged me in a friendly conversation in the lawn outside. I had seen some of them prompting some people to heckle me. But now their tone was conciliatory. I soon discovered that they had no ill-will against me, and were basically of amiable disposition.

"Jagmohanji," so the gist of their talk went, "people of Delhi are generally appreciative of what you have done in regard to planning and development of the city. You have taken a bold stand. You have been coming all alone to appear before the Commission. We have ourselves been heckling you. But you have stuck to your stand gamely. We appreciate all this. We commend your courage and stoic calm. But one thing we do not understand. Why don't you name Sanjay Gandhi?"

"My dear friends," I replied, "You are mistaken. I am stating what in essence is the truth. I am not interested in politics and power structure. Nor am I shielding anyone. No one coerced me to do anything. You are assuming that something wrong was done. In fact, what was done was in the interest of the poor, in the interest of the city's development. I had no doubt about it. The programme discarded superficial humanism which was merely a cloak to conceal political and other vested interests. It restored the balance of values. It demostrated that those who violated laws would not get preference over those who respected them. During the proceedings of the Commission, has it not occurred to you that the moral fibre of the community has been so viciously eroded that not a single person submitted either a layout plan or a building plan to any authority, what to speak of getting it actually sanctioned?

"Let us face the truth. I got the schemes of clearance and resettlement executed because I believed in their intrinsic merit. I saw in them real humanism, real justice—justice not only to the individuals but also to the community. All those who are today saying that they were forced to carry out clearance were earlier singing songs in praise of what was done. This is morally nauseating. It also shows that they did something in which they themselves did not believe. In other words, they were untrue to themselves. I ask you, if a person is not true to himself, would he be true to the society, true to the state?

"Unfortunately, we are missing the central issues and going to peripheral ones. Unless we learn to insulate slums from politics and adopt a non-political approach to basic civic issues our cities will remain ugly and disorganized. They will continue to provide excellent material for denigration to a Katherine Mayo, a Renold Segal, a Naipaul, a Louise Malle."

My reply was, perhaps, much longer than what was expected. I noticed that the atmosphere was getting a little tense. To relieve the tension, I struck a lighter tone. I recited to them the following lines of Goethe about Napoleon:

On Judgment Day, before God's throne,
There stood at last, Napoleon.
The Devil had his list begun
Of Crimes the Bonaparts had done,
When God the Father, or God the Son,
Cut Satan short before God's throne:
"Don't bore us all to death with reading
A German professorial pleading!
If you're bold enough to face him,
In your kingdom you may place him.

They laughed, shook hands, and parted company. I found them friendly and sporting. But on 22 April 1978, I saw blood in the eyes of some of those young men, when there was a virtual riot in the Commission's room for about half an hour before the commencement of the proceedings. Chairs were hurled, filthy abuses were showered. The entire atmosphere was surcharged with conflict and hostility. Where were we heading to? Riots in the Commission's room!

Things have really fallen apart. The power struggle has led us to the blind alley. We seem to be picking up the wrong end of the stick, and confusing development with destruction, justice with technicality, dynamism with ruthlessness, humanism with brutality. The areas of darkness, of which we have never been free, are becoming thicker and thicker. The mental slums have gripped us and paralyzed our will to act in the right direction. It is time that we clear these slums, stop flogging the dead corpse of symptoms, attend to the microbes that spread the infection, and set ourselves the fundamental task of curing the "disease that afflicts us all."

CHAPTER VIII

UNTOLD STORY OF TURKMAN GATE

Truth is the best tactics
because it excludes tactics
IVAN SVITAK

Turkman Gate derives its name from Shah Turkman, a famous saint, who died on 19 February 1240 A.D. His real name was Shames-ul-Arifin. He was also called Biyabani, a man of forests and wilderness, a recluse. His tomb, a white marble grave, is located within a graveyard of Turkman Gate in which there are a number of brick-built graves, presumed to be those of the saint's followers.

It is fairly certain that the site, where Turkman Gate now stands, was the bank of the Yamuna in the thirteenth century. This is borne out of the fact that the grave of Queen Razia Sultana (1236-1239), who was buried on the bank of the river, is located near Turkman Gate. Not far from the site, an incomplete city was founded by Mubarak Shah in 1344 at a site lying between Ajmeri Gate and Turkman Gate. He died before any construction could take place.

In 1638, the Mughal emperor Shahjahan decided to shift his headquarters from Agra and build a new Capital on the bank of the Yamuna. Here, a huge, massive Red Fort, with its mighty walls, gates, towers, and battlements, was constructed in about eight years. The Fort was almost a self-contained imperial township, accommodating about 5,000 persons. In course of time, a city grew around the Red Fort with a protective wall which was a special feature of the medieval cities. The wall was completed during Aurangzeb's time. It had a number of gates. Turkman Gate was one of them.

The Turkman Gate incident (19 April 1976) was unfortunate. It resulted in loss of six lives. But the incident, as would be evident from the following facts, was not caused by the

DDA's drive to clear slum and squatter settlements. The amount of falsehood, fiction, and exaggeration that has been woven around it must have anguished the soul of saint Turkman who, knowing the ways of the world and the excesses which a society in troubled times was capable of committing on individuals, kept himself aloof from the public. Queen Razia, in her neglected grave, must also have wondered whether she was the only one who suffered on account of intrigue and deception.

The extent of exaggeration can be judged from the fact that Kuldip Nayar in his widely-circulated book, *The Judgement*, gave the number of dead in Turkman Gate as 150, and the number of houses demolished as 1,000—the former was exaggerated by 25 times, and the latter by eight times. The 120 houses cleared by the DDA belonged to it and had been legally declared dangerous and unfit for human habitation. In other words, the impression that private houses were demolished is exaggerated 1,000 times. Being in a hurry, Kuldip Nayar had no time to check facts, and was presumably misled by persons like Inder Mohan who himself gave the figure of dead in Turkman Gate as 300.

Now, I shall deal with the context, the reality, the untold story of records and resolutions, of acquisitions and allotments, of truth and justice in its essence, shorn of its narrowness and technicality.

BACKGROUND

A pocket of about seven acres, near Turkman Gate, was cleared of the slums—dangerous and dilapidated—in the clearance-cum-resettlement operations beginning from 13 April 1976 and ending on 27 April 1976. This pocket alongwith the other area, known as Delhi Ajmeri Gate area, was in an unhealthy and unhygienic state.

An improvement/redevelopment scheme was formulated for the aforesaid area as early as 1938 vide Delhi Improvement Trust's Resolution No. 200 of 28 February 1938. This Resolution, inter alia, stated as under:

> The necessity to alleviate slum conditions behind city wall between the Delhi Gate and Ajmeri Gate has burdened the official and public conscience for at least 12 years, but so far

without result. . . .

The effect of unhealthy condition of life is demonstrated by the statistics of tuberculosis, infantile mortality and enteric fever. . . .

The Trust ought to frame an improvement scheme, in view of the fact that, in an area extending upto about 400 ft. behind the wall between Delhi Gate and Ajmeri Gate, (1) a number of buildings used as dwelling places are unfit for human habitations; (2) danger to the health of inhabitants in the area is caused by the narrowness of streets, and closeness, bad arrangement of houses, also by the want of light, air, ventilation and adequate sanitary conveniences.

On the basis of this Resolution, an improvement scheme/Land Acquisition Notification was issued and published in the Government of India *Gazette* on 19 March 1938. It was published in the government's *Gazette* of 26 March 1938 and 2 April 1938.

The sanction of the entire improvement scheme was accorded by the Competent Authority (Chief Commissioner), and published in the government's *Gazette* of 4 May 1946. The relevant notification, No. F. 1(95)/45-L.G., dated 29 April 1946 read, inter alia, as under:

It is hereby notified for general information that the Chief Commissioner of Delhi has sanctioned the improvement scheme known as the "Delhi Ajmere Gate Slum Clearance Scheme" framed by the Delhi Development Authority.

The pocket of seven acres of land, in question, was covered by the Improvement Trust's Resolution, the improvement scheme/Land Acquisition Notification, and the Chief Commissioner's sanction.

Subsequently, after coming into force of the Slum Areas (Improvement and Clearance) Act, 1956, a notification, dated 24 April 1957, was issued, declaring the entire area of Delhi Ajmeri Gate Scheme as slum area. The notification described the area as "unfit for human habitation and detrimental to safety, health, etc."

In 1960, the slum clearance work was entrusted by the central government to the Delhi Municipal Corporation. From 1960 to February 1974, this work remained with the Corporation.

In the government and other quarters, an impression was formed that the slum clearance work had not been handled properly by the Delhi Municipal Corporation and a number of old schemes remained unimplemented and hundreds of tenements built with the funds made available for slum clearance scheme were either lying vacant or had been unauthorizedly occupied. The Public Accounts Committee of Parliament is also understood to have commented adversely on the subject.

Following the report submitted to the central government in June 1973 by the then Lieutenant Governor, Baleshwar Prasad, about the unsatisfactory handling of the slum clearance work by the Delhi Municipal Corporation and the long pendency of the old schemes, like the one in question, the slum clearance work was transferred in February 1974, by the central government from the Delhi Municipal Corporation to the DDA. Evidently, the purpose of the transfer was to secure speedy and expeditious implementation of the slum clearance schemes and the connected projects. The DDA did not ask for the transfer. It was the central government which entrusted the slum clearance work to it.

In pursuance of the sanctioned scheme of Delhi Ajmeri Gate area, the properties were acquired and a number of awards were drawn up in 1948, 1949, 1950, 1951, and 1952. The possession was taken in mid-fifties. The "Nazul"/government land as well as the lands belonging to erstwhile Delhi Municipal Committee were either purchased by the Delhi Improvement Trust or got transferred for the purpose of execution of the scheme. Some properties in the area, which belonged to the custodian, were obtained by transfer from the Ministry of Rehabilitation in early sixties, on payment of compensation calculated in terms of the provision of the Slum Areas (Improvement and Clearance) Act, 1956.

The basic objective was to execute a compact and comprehensive slum clearance scheme and redevelop the area. Unfortunately, due to various reasons, including pressure of vested interest and administrative apathy and indifference and the tendency to follow the least line of resistence, the scheme remained unexecuted for over 30 years. The long neglect and pendency of the case created its own complications, particularly in regard to non-maintenance of proper records, and added to the problems of implementation. Is it not ironical that those who did practically nothing for over 30 years are not being questioned?

In 1969-70, the Delhi Municipal Corporation reconsidered the scheme and approved the revised pattern of development, and also divided the occupants of properties in two categories—unauthorized and authorized. The Corporation, inter alia, stipulated that unauthorized occupants were not entitled to any alternative accommodation, while the authorized occupants should be allotted flats elsewhere and brought back to the site after redevelopment and reconstruction.

While carrying out the clearance-cum-resettlement operations in the pocket of the land in question, the above referred decisions were broadly followed by the DDA. In fact, a comparatively more liberal approach was adopted and alternative plots—both residential and commercial—were allotted even to the unauthorized occupants, including the recent ones, without even charging any damages for the period of unauthorized occupation.

We had no doubt that voluntarily and willing shifting would be secured if the following incentives and inducements were given:

(i) Those who continued to occupy properties even after acquisition or those who had been paying rent or "damages" would be given tenements in Ranjit Nagar near Patel Nagar.

(ii) Those who were rank squatters and had no semblance of authority whatsoever and were not entitled to any alternative accommodation under the Resolution passed by the then Competent Authority, viz Delhi Municipal Corporation, would be given plots in the resettlement colonies of Trilokpuri and Nand Nagri. (For the surplus population, such as squatters and unauthorized occupants, the Seminar on the Redevelopment of Shahjahanabad, held in February 1975, had recommended resettlement in the trans-Yamuna area. These recommendations had been accepted by the central government.)

(iii) Those who wished to take flats built by the DDA under Low or Middle-Income Group Housing Schemes would be allotted those flats by relaxing the normal conditions of registration and participation in the draw of lots.

(*iv*) Since the houses had been declared slums and were acquired long ago and the records had been changing from office to office, compensation would be paid under the Slum Clearance Act in all those cases where there was any doubt about the ownership of the property and where any worthwhile proof of ownership could be given.

The clearance operation commenced on 13 April 1976 proceeded smoothly and peacefully. On 19 April 1976, however, there was a riot in the area—in our view, entirely due to family planning campaign and incitement by vested interests. The firing was resorted to under the orders of magistracy/police and there were some casualties. The DDA carried out hundreds of clearance-cum-resettlement operations both before and during the emergency and there was no disturbances anywhere—not even a gesture of violence.

The correct position, in brief, is:

(*i*) The physical and environmental conditions of life in the slum pocket in question were sub-human. The continued habitation in these buildings would not only have been injurious to health but also dangerous to life.

(*ii*) The clearance-cum-resettlement was taken up in accordance with the policy and thinking of the government on the subject.

(*iii*) Following long delay in the implementation of the slum clearance scheme by the Delhi Municipal Corporation, the central government, on the report of the then Lieutenant Governor, Baleshwar Prasad, decided to transfer the slum clearance work to the DDA with the expectation that the slum clearance work would not remain on paper alone and would be implemented speedily. The DDA basically implemented the decision taken by the Corporation vide its Resolution No. 559/C&C, dated 21 July 1969/70, after making it more liberal in respect of allotment of alternative accommodation. In reality, no fresh decision was taken.

(*iv*) The procedure and practice adopted in the "demolition"/clearance-cum-resettlement operation of the pocket in question was the same as was followed in similar other operations which were carried out by the DDA shortly before the emergency or during the emergency but before the operation in question.

(*v*) The clearance-cum-resettlement operation was carried out slowly and smoothly, and there was no attempt to hustle through, as would be evident from the fact that the operation was spread over a long span of time, i.e. from 13 April 1976 to 27 April 1976, although the number of buildings to be handled was not large. There was some lack of clarity in respect of property registers due to long neglect and pendency of the case, but there were really no private buildings involved in the "demolition" and no worthwhile proof was given in support of any claim of ownership.

(*vi*) The rioting and subsequent firing was due to the strong emotional reaction to the family planning campaign and incitement by certain interests.

(*vii*) The deployment of the police force was in accordance with the instructions of the Lieutenant Governor issued in 1967 and similar deployment was done in practically all major clearance operations undertaken before the emergency.

(*viii*) Bulldozers were used as a labour-saving technique and for clearing the debris speedily and pulling down the vacated buildings from which window and door frames and other salvageable building material had already been taken by the previous squatters and slum-dwellers. This practice, too, has been in vogue for the last one or two decades. Free transport was provided to the families effected for carrying their belongings as well as building material.

It was a simple slum clearance and resettlement scheme, duly approved by the competent authority, and executed with due regard to changed circumstances. The procedure and practices adopted were the same as were adopted in similar other operations carried out by the DDA before and during the emergency. The administrative lapses and procedural deficiency, if any, were, to a large extent, inherent in the execution of the scheme that remained pending for over three decades. There have been absolutely no wilful demolition.

Why Was the Clearance Operation Taken Up?

The physical conditions of the area in question were so bad that a scheme for its redevelopment was prepared by the Delhi Improvement Trust about 40 years ago. This is what is recorded in original Resolution No. 200, dated 28 February 1938:

> Behind the pleasant lawns and imposing structure of the city wall, which form the boundary to New Delhi, lie squalid, over-crowded, ill-ventilated and ill-serviced houses, nonetheless present and shameful because not generally seen. The area comprise Municipal Wards VIII and X for which the *Hume Report* gave the following figures of over-crowding:

Ward Number	1931 census circles	Intensity of population in built over area (person per acre)	Excess according to standard proposed in the report
VIII	216, 217	389	2,577
	218, 219	398	2,187
	221, 222	349	2,094
	223	332	1,493
			8,351
X	233	290	1,069
	234, 235	270	1,180
	236	490	1,173
			3,422

Conditions

In 1954, Jawaharlal Nehru visited the area. He was horrified by the conditions of living and involuntarily cried: "Burn them!" After coming into force of the Slum Areas (Improvement and Clearance) Act, 1956, a notification was issued on 20 April 1957, declaring the area as slum area, i.e. the area comprising mostly the dilapidated, dangerous, congested, and insanitary buildings.

With mounting pressure on space, the physical and environmental conditions of the area, which was declared as slum area about four decades ago, can be well imagined. It was virtually a hell hole, a cemetery of living men, with disease and disability hovering all around. For instance, in one single unit, with crumbling walls and roofs and with electric wiring precariously bulging out, as many as 30 families, with a population of about 200 persons, were living. The average size of the family in this area was 6.47. About 32 per cent families had eight or more children.[1]

Marshal Clinand, a noted American sociologist, who visited Delhi slums in the late 1950s, had this to say:

> Houses are one and two storey, so close together that no sun comes through, everything is damp and this makes the odours of filth and urine all the more noticeable. There is an awful stench everywhere. The area was covered with hordes of flies. Children use the gutters. Saw a man eating his lunch in front of his house a yard away from flies and offal in the gutter. I almost threw up, and the educated Indians with me put their handkerchief over their faces. The children have only one small place to play, and it is in bad condition. . . .
>
> As we drove away I kept the windows up so that the hordes of flies would not get inside. *I couldn't eat my lunch that day.* . . . Had a feeling as though I had seen enough and wanted to forget the misery. . . .[2]

To bring home the conditions of congestion and chaos, I may take the liberty of quoting from my book, *Rebuilding Shahjahanabad: The Walled City of Delhi:*

> Shahjahanabad is a gem with many facets, some dark, some bright. Unfortunately, it is the darker side which has gained predominance and bright spots of Shahjahanabad's social and cultural life are getting submerged in the dust and debris of the new forces. Swamped by the flow of migrants after 1947 and mauled badly by the ruthless violation of the municipal bye-laws, Shahjahanabad stands before us today as a battered, sick, and over-burdened city. It seems to have lost its centre, its soul. It appears even insensitive to pain. Most of the residents are not even conscious of the filth and odour around them. Such is their tragedy. Such is the culture of poverty, degradation, and indifference that breeds in

Shahjahanabad today.

In the Draft Zonal Plan of the area, formulated under the provisions of the Delhi Master Plan, the pocket in question had been described as "clearance area," i.e. area to be demolished and redeveloped.

In the immediate vicinity of the pocket cleared, i.e. Gali Ismile Khan (Turkman Gate) and Kucha Pati Ram, seven persons died and eight injured in the two recent house collapses. An extract from a report of the *Hindustan Times* (6 August 1977) is given below:

> Two persons were killed and three injured when the roof of a house under repair in Gali Ismile Khan, Mohalla Kabristan, near Turkman Gate collapsed this morning.
>
> With today's tragedy, the monsoon toll this season has gone up to eight and the tally of injured stands at 44.
>
> The house adjacent to the collapsed one has also been declared dangerous. Another roof of a house in Bazar Sita Ram also collapsed last night. But nobody was injured.

There was a real risk to life in living in the dilapidated and dangerous buildings of the type demolished in the clearance operation. Subsequent fate of the occupants of similar buildings in the vicinity of the area cleared leave hardly any room for challenging this view.

The above facts clearly show that the physical and environmental conditions of the area justified the execution of the demolition/clearance-cum-resettlement operation. There were also other valid grounds for doing so.

Transfer

During 1960-74, the slum clearance work remained with the Delhi Municipal Corporation. The then Lieutenant Governor, Baleshwar Prasad, was not satisfied with the performance of the Delhi Municipal Corporation and recommended to the central government in June 1973 that the work should be transferred to the DDA. After consideration of the Lieutenant Governor's report, the government decided that the slum clearance work should be transferred from the Delhi Municipal Corporation to the DDA, so that pending schemes were implemented speedily and tenements built with the funds sanctioned by Parliament for slum clearance work were allotted to the bonafide slum-dwellers. Another consideration that was implied in the transfer was that the DDA was already dealing with the clearance of squatters from public lands, and it could effectively deal with the clearance work in the area where both the squatters and bonafide slum-dwellers were inter-mixed. This could be done by providing alternative accommodation in the shape of tenements to those who were covered by the Slum Clearance Scheme and by taking care of the squatters under the Squatter Resettlement Scheme. It was also thought that those slum-dwellers whose economic conditions had improved and did not wish to move to the tenements built under the Slum Clearance Scheme could be persuaded by the DDA to shift to any of its Janta, Low and Middle Income Group houses built under its public housing schemes.

If the expectation which the government entertained at the time of transfer of the slum clearance work to the DDA were to be realized, it was necessary for the DDA to take up the old pending projects of slum clearance and execute the schemes as speedily as feasible and to make early use of the vacant or unauthorizedly occupied tenements built for the bonafide slum-dwellers. The Delhi Ajmeri Gate Scheme, in which the "cleared-pocket" fell, was the oldest scheme, and it was quite natural that at least some portion of it facing Asaf Ali Road should be taken up for clearance and redevelopment.

A large number of tenements built under the Slum Clearance Scheme with the funds sanctioned for the specific purpose by Parliament had either been lying unutilized or allotted to persons ineligible for allotment of such tenements. This was obviously unsatisfactory. First, the meagre funds allocated for slum clearance work were not being properly utilized, and national resources, both in terms of money and scarce building material, were being wasted. Secondly, no slum area was being cleared while physical and environmental conditions continued to deteriorate, thereby exposing the inhabitants to serious health hazard and physical danger inherent in the occupancy of dilapidated buildings.

In April 1976, i.e. the time when the clearance of the area was contemplated, about 1,500 tenements built for the slum clearance projects were lying vacant and another 600 were in occupation of ineligible persons. The particulars of those tenements are:

Sl. No	Locality	No. of tenements lying vacant on 1 April 1976	No. of tenements in occupation of the unauthorized persons
1	2	3	4
1.	Inderlok	922	—
2.	Rajit Nagar/near Patel Nagar	160	480
3.	Bagh Kare Khan	75	120
4.	Shahdara G.T.	39	—
5.	Mata Sundri Road	9	—
6.	Moti Nagar	—	264
7.	Other colonies	288	—
	Total	1,493	864

It is obvious that, in the context of the mounting cost of construction of buildings, the cost of the tenements referred in the above table would be considerably lower than the cost of tenements to be built subsequently. Consequently, their rents and their purchase price would be lower. (The eligible allottees have the option to purchase these tenements by paying hire-purchase instalment spread over a period of 20 years.)

Whom should these vacant tenements, carrying lower rents and purchase prices, have been allotted? Obviously, the eligible slum-dwellers of the old schemes, like those of the land in question, deserved to be given preference, particularly when these tenements were close to the newly developed industrial and warehousing units, where old industries and trades had been shifted from the congested areas of the city according to the provisions of the Master Plan. This factor constituted another justification for taking up the clearance work.

LOCATION AND PRIORITY

The pocket of the land cleared was located in between the two well-developed commercial areas of Asaf Ali Road. This pocket, with old and dilapidated buildings, inter-mixed with petty commercial establishments, godowns, coal depots and the like, was an eyesore. Anyone passing through Asaf Ali Road was struck by the sad spectacle of an ugly slum. To give priority to this pocket in the sphere of slum clearance work was in the natural order of things.

The work of slum clearance had not been suddenly taken up. Before the clearance of the pocket of land in question a number of clearance-cum-resettlement operation in respect of the built-up slum areas had been undertaken by the DDA. The particulars of seven built-up slums, which were cleared by demolishing the properties and resettling the occupants in tenements or plots, are given in the table on next page.

In Chapter IV, relating to the clearance-cum-resettlement operations during the emergency, it has been indicated how a high-level decision had been taken by the government to shift slum and squatter settlements and non-conforming trades, and how the government policy, programme, and thinking on the subject was made clear and reinforced in the statements made by the Prime Minister and the Minister of Works and Housing in Parliament and also by the Chief Executive Councillor of the Delhi Metropolitan Council. In view of this policy, was their anything wrong in taking up this clearance operation?

PROCEDURES AND PRECEDENTS

As regards the procedures followed, the normal practice in Delhi had been to shift the squatters and slum-dwellers through incentive and inducement. This practice is particularly in vogue in the case of properties/lands owned by the government and public authorities. Application of Public Premises Act, for instance, neither yields practical results nor affords any real relief to the unauthorized occupants of public land and properties. Apart from the fact that this Act does not provide them alternative accommodation, it subjects unauthorized occupant to the payment of damages at the market rate and involves him in litigation. In practice, too, it is impossible to pass eviction order simultaneously against all the unauthorized occupants of a particular building or site and thus secure vacant possession of the

Sl. No.	Name of the property	Time of clearance	No. of families involved	Localities where shifted	Remarks
1	2	3	4	5	6
1.	4090-4094/XII Katra Meena Bagh	June-July 74	140	Sarai Rohilla, Moti Nagar, Ranjit Nagar	Ranjit Nagar is the colony where the slum-dwellers of Turkman Gate were resettled
2.	7523/XV, Katra Kareem Khan Paharganj	July-August 74	150	Ranjit Nagar	
3.	416/XIV Sarai Rohilla	September 74	25	Moti Nagar	Moti Nagar is at considerable distance from Sarai Rohilla
4.	Other small properties numbering about 12	July-August 74	100	Moti Nagar, Ranjit Nagar, Sarai Rohilla	
5.	Katra Sheesh Mahal	April 1975	630	Mata Sundri Road	(This is an exact precedent to what was done to the occupants of properties in Turkman Gate area)
6.	Kalan Mahal, Directorate of Education, Delhi Administration, Delhi	April 1976	50	The occupants (39) who had some semblance of authority were given tenements in Mata Sundri Road while the rank squatters (62) were given plots in the resettlement colony of Seelampur	
7.	Families from Paharganj	1975		Moti Nagar	Moti Nagar tenements are at considerable*

*Distance from Pahar Ganj.

entire building or site at the same time. In view of these considerations, it has always been the practice with public authorities to secure possession of the public land and properties through inducements and incentives.

Care has, however, to be taken to ensure that inducement and incentive do not become so attractive that they encourage large-scale unauthorized occupation of public lands and properties. If, for instance, an unauthorized occupant of public property in slum area, who is not eligible for allotment under Slum Clearance Scheme, is allotted a flat, it will result in further unauthorized occupation of public properties, thereby causing further deterioration in the conditions of living. It will also deprive the eligible family of the chance to secure early allotment of tenement and move out of the slum. In fact, the dilemma of the public authorities dealing with the problem of slums is: if liberal treatment is adopted it brings in a flood of new migrants—squatters and slum-dwellers—and renders the problem incapable of solution; if, on the other hand, such treatment is denied the question of human consideration and conscience arise.

Before taking up the clearance in the area in question, a number of clearance-cum-resettlement operations in the slum areas had been undertaken by the DDA before the emergency under the instructions and supervision of the then Commissioner (Slums), P.P. Srivastava. These clearance operations included Katra Meena Bagh, Katra Karim, Katra Sheesh Mahal, Kalan Mahal and properties bearing numbers:

1. XVIII/416
2. XIII/421
3. XII/3792
4. XII/3798
5. XII/4609
6. XII/4090-94
   plus 3595-3608
7. XII/18504
8. XII/8085
9. XII/8608
10. XV/9346-50
11. XV/9330-34
12. XV/7893-94

The procedures and practice adopted in these operations were the precedents for the procedures and practice adopted by the slum staff of the DDA deputed for the task.

In executing the clearance-cum-resettlement operations of the pocket of land in question, the prevailing procedure of offering inducements and incentives was adopted. In this pocket, there were two categories of families: (*a*) Families who continued to occupy the properties even after acquisition or who were shifted from Dujana House in the transit camp built 12 years ago or had some semblance of authority for occupation and were paying rent or damages. (These families were categorized as "authorized" for alternative allotment.) (*b*) Families who were squatters, and were not paying rent or damages. (These families were categorized as "unauthorized" for the purpose of alternative allotment.)

Here, it is necessary to invite attention again to the Delhi Municipal Corporation Resolution No. 959/C&C, dated 21 July 1969. This resolution was passed when the scheme of Delhi Ajmeri Gate was with the Corporation. It is interesting to note that those who are today criticizing the clearance were themselves responsible for passing the resolution in which it was stipulated that unauthorized occupants, that is, those who were not paying any rent or damages, were not entitled to alternative accommodation. The resolution laid down:

(*i*) The "authorized families", i.e. families falling in category (*a*), should be shifted temporarily to the available slum tenements outside and then settled permanently on the cleared site after its redevelopment.

(*ii*) There is no legal liability to provide alternative accommodation to "unauthorized families" even if they were regularized as licencees in accordance with the recent decision of the Ad-hoc (Slum Clearance and Improvement) Committee. Thus, the families falling in category (*b*) were not entitled to any alternative accommodation even if they got unauthorized occupation regularized by paying licence fee.

In its report of 14 November 1975 the Slum Department of the DDA made it clear, "there is no legal binding to provide alternative accommodation to the unauthorised families."

In the clearance-cum-resettlement project executed in April 1976, more liberal treatment was accorded to both categories (*a*) and (*b*) than was envisaged under the Corporation Resolution, so that this could act as an incentive for voluntary and willing shifting.

The position in respect of these two categories need to be explained separately.

CATEGORY (*a*)

About 1500 tenements built with the funds sanctioned for the slum clearance work were lying vacant in April 1976. Out of these, the most attractive tenements were in Ranjit Nagar. This was because of the following reasons:

(*i*) Ranjit Nagar is very near the much sought after residential colonies of Patel Nagar and Naraina, where land values and rents are very high.

(*ii*) In accordance with the provisions of the Delhi Master Plan, new industrial and warehousing colonies had been developed by the DDA in Maya Puri (Phase I and Phase II) and Naraina (Phase I and Phase II). In these colonies, which are very near to Ranjit Nagar, a large number of new industrial and warehousing units had come up, in addition to thousands of industrial and warehousing units which have been shifted from the old city in accordance with the provision of the Delhi Master Plan. These units included iron-merchant market, machinery merchant market, kabari and wood market, etc. The number of units functioning in these colonies is over 1,000. These units provided extensive employment opportunities, particularly to the category of the families in question.

(*iii*) The cost of the tenements built in Ranjit Nagar was low. Consequently, the rent to be charged from the allottees was comparatively low. It was only Rs 22 per month. As against this, the rent of tenements in Mata Sundri-Minto Road Complex was Rs 73.5. (This was, however, subsequently reduced to Rs 51 per month.) Likewise, the purchase price of Ranjit Nagar tenements, which is worked out by capitalizing the rental value, was considerably lower than the purchase price of tenements in Mata Sundri-Minto Road Complex.

Thus, from the point of view of environment, location, rent, employment opportunities, and future potential, the Ranjit Nagar tenements were ideal. When the offer of allotment of these flats was made to the families of category (*a*), they accepted[3] it and voluntarily moved out of the Turkman Gate slums to settle in the new tenements. An added attraction was the allotment of the tenements to the families with larger members.

Some of the families of category (*a*) opted for allotment of tenements in Shahdara mainly due to personal reasons and still cheaper rates of rent (Rs 13.50 per month) and consequently lower purchase price. Allotment of one tenement was made in Mata Sundri Road on compassionate grounds.

Thus, the total number of families of category (*a*) allotted tenements was 183 (145 in Ranjit Nagar, 37 in Shahdara, and one in Mata Sundri Road).

Within the ambit of the scheme and in the context of the prevailing conditions, nothing could be more liberal and more attractive than this treatment. None of the families allotted flats in the above areas expressed any desire to return if the vacated area was to be used for constructing residential units. This was because of the changed circumstances and shifting of old industries and trades to the new industrial and warehousing units near Ranjit Nagar. If, however, any family wanted to return it could be accommodated in the tenements to be built subsequently in the cleared site if it was to be used for residential purposes, or in the Minto Road-Mata Sundri Complex as and when allotment of additional land was made by the government to the DDA.

Category (*b*)

In terms of the Corporation resolution, families falling in category (*b*), "squatters/unauthorized persons," were not entitled to any alternative accommodation. In taking this decision, the Delhi Municipal Corporation, and for that matter any public authority, would naturally be influenced by the consideration that any concession to the squatters would add to the problem of squatting, encourage unauthorized occupation and non-payment of rent or damages, and also affect adversely the interest of the bonafide slum-dwellers eligible for allotment under the Slum Clearance Scheme.

Families of this category were aware that they were not entitled to any allotment of alternative accommodation, particularly when they had not even cared to get their occupation regularized by paying licence fee. They, therefore, reacted favourably to the idea of getting alternative plots and shifting to the new resettlement colonies across the Yamuna, which were fast developing and in which 18,000 families, involving a population of about 1 lakh, had already been settled.

Our decision to allot alternative plots even to "unauthorized persons" was influenced by humanitarian considerations. To make this incentive more attractive and to minimize the temporary hardship inherent in shifting it was also decided that:

(*i*) No question about the period of unauthorized occupation would be asked and no damages, whicn have to be levied on the basis of the market value, would be collected

(*ii*) Larger families would be provided additional plots.

(*iii*) In addition to the residential plots, commercial plots would be allotted to those who were running some petty shops within their houses or outside.

(*iv*) Even the latest arrival (squatter family) would be given alternative accommodation

(*v*) Free transport would be provided and families allowed to take salvageable building material on the trucks provided by the DDA

(*vi*) Those who wish to take DDA flats built in the newly developed areas under its public housing schemes for Low and Middle Income Groups could do so and secure allotment of houses in the colony of their choice without complying with the normal requirement of registration and allotment through lots.

The concessions and incentives provided strong inducement to shift to the new resettlement colonies where there was security of tenure and distinct possibility of becoming owners of the plots and also securing loans for construction or improvement of their houses.

The unhealthy physical conditions of the area and dilapidated and dangerous conditions of the buildings had instilled an incipient desire in the minds of the occupants to vacate these buildings. This contention is supported by the fact that merely in response to DDA's press advertisements (August-September 1976) advising the occupants of dilapidated and dangerous buildings to shift, about 700 occupants of such buildings in the nearby buildings of Chowk Shah Mubarak and Hanuman Garh moved out of their buildings and secured allotment from the DDA.

In Sarai Khalil, too, the shifting was voluntary, and people came to obtain allotment slips from its camp office set up for this purpose in Pahar Ganj. In this operation, acquisition of a built-up private property was involved and this acquisition was approved by the Lieutenant Governor. The inmates of these private properties themselves wanted to move out of this slum.

In Gali Khane Khana area also, the shifting was totally voluntary. G.C. Srivastava, Deputy Commissioner (Slums), an officer other than the one who was in charge of the Turkman Gate area, reported: "By the local residents, the area behind Fish Market was suggested for clearance. . . . As per local residents, all these people were willing to shift to Ranjit Nagar. The number of families to be shifted will be 250. . . . We have received requests even from neighbouring areas."

It is quite clear from the above observations that occupants of the old slum properties were quite willing to move out. Some of them were even keen to do so. There was a general trend in favour of shifting.

The above contention is further supported by the subsequent requests received from various occupants of similar buildings in the locality. In this regard, it is relevant to quote from the recent application, dated 1 August 1977, sent to various authorities by the occupants of Katra Daulat Ram, Turkman Gate:

> Presently, we are living in a deplorable and scornful position due to unhealthy atmosphere. There is suffocation and congestion due to large population. It is a tiny hell on the earth. There is foul smell in the atmosphere. Mosquitoes breed their

eggs on the heaps of the dirt which spread malaria fever and other chronic diseases. Many persons have been suffering from T.B., asthma and other diseases.

Houses have been constructed in disorderly manner, with kacha sand and weak materials. There is no ventilators, windows and exhaust for throwing bad smell out of the house. *No human being can live in these houses.* The life of these houses is over and may collapse at any time. Most of the houses are in dangerous condition and we fear that they may not collapse during this rainy season.

In view of the above noted circumstances, we hope that our DDA and our ruling Government in the hands of Janta Party may consider our grievances on priority basis and arrange immediately to shift us from this hell and get rid of us from the ensuing calamities of the nature. . . .

This clearly shows that the occupants of the buildings like those of the cleared site realized the risk of their health and life inherent in the continued habitation of such buildings. That this risk was real is confirmed by the fact that in the immediate vicinity of the pocket cleared by the DDA, seven persons died and eight injured in July 1977 when two houses collapsed near Turkman Gate in Gali Ismile Khan and Kucha Pati Ram. It was realization of risks involved that had created an incipient desire to shift to the new areas. At least there was no disinclination to shift and when very attractive incentives and inducements were provided, shifting took place. The fact that persuasion had worked would be evident from the smooth and steady manner in which the families came to the camping office of the DDA, obtained their demolition/allotment slips, and signed or thumb-marked it, obtained trucks and moved according to their convenience. The area to be cleared had been indicated on the site plan and the street was made the boundary to facilitate easy understanding of the area to be cleared.

At the present juncture, it is difficult to imagine the general mood of the squatters and slum-dwellers and their level of aspiration at the time of clearance, especially in April 1976. They were not at all unwilling to move to the new resettlement colonies because of the alternative allotments and other inducements and the general feeling that at the site of present occupation, they would always feel uncertain about their future, and be subjected to various types of problems. It was because of subsequent promises made at the time of elections that the level of aspiration of slum-dwellers and squatters changed radically. Now everybody has been promised accommodation in the heart of the city, as if seven lakhs people could be accommodated in the "heart"!

It has been alleged that the families of category (b) were allotted land in the distant colonies of Trilokpuri-Khichripur and Nand Nagri, where employment opportunities were low and civic amenities did not exist. The allegations are not correct.

When the families of category (b) were allotted alternative sites in Trilokpuri-Khichripuri complex, it was no wilderness. Before April 1976, 8,100 families, involving a population of 40,000, were living in this complex, with facilities of sufficiently high order. Likewise, in Nand Nagri 8,900 families had been settled before the families from Turkman Gate area moved in. (Allotments in Nand Nagri or Trilokpuri complex were made according to the choice of the allottees.)

Special attention was paid to the resettlement colonies. The extent of work done, the amenities provided, and the employment opportunities created have already been detailed in Chapters I to V. According to Delhi Development Authority's Town Planner's report of 14 November 1975, occupations of 50 per cent of the families was such that they could be settled anywhere.

Our method, it would be seen, was to provide incentives and inducements and give liberal treatment, both at the time of shifting and in the resettlement sites. These are the real factors which help the squatters and slum-dwellers. From a technical point, too, the competent authority is competent to order the demolition under Section 13 of the Slum Areas (Improvement and Clearance) Act, 1956, because the properties in question had been acquired, and belonged to the central government. This section reads:

> Where any land in a slum area or clearance area has been acquired under this Act the Central Govt. shall make the land available to the Competent Authority for the purpose of executing any work of improvement or carrying out any work of demolition or for the purpose of re-development.

Untold Story of Turkman Gate

In this case the properties had been acquired by the Delhi Improvement Trust for the slum clearance project and vested in the central government after the dissolution of Trust. Thereafter, the central government gave these properties to the DDA for slum clearance work. The properties transferred by the Ministry of Rehabilitation were also central government properties and their cost was paid by the DDA in terms of the provisions of the Slum Clearance Act and they have, therefore, to be treated as properties given to the DDA by the central government for the slum clearance work. The Nazul properties in the area were also transferred to the DDA for the same purpose. The competent authority of the DDA could, therefore, pass the necessary order of demolition. Apart from the fact that, in view of the voluntary shifting or shifting for consideration, no formal notice was required, Section 13 of the Slum Clearance Act does not provide for any notice. After all, what is the basic purpose of a notice? It is to facilitate the occupant to make alternative arrangements. In the case of the type in question, arrangement for alternative accommodation could not be made by the occupants themselves and such arrangements were made by the DDA staff. Transport arrangements had also been made by the DDA. It was not compulsory to move on the same day. The allottees usually took their own time.

The provisions for Sections 9 and 10 are applicable only when properties to be cleared are private and their acquisition is to be done subsequently or no willing and voluntary shifting can be secured through incentives and inducements.

The concessions, incentives, and inducements extended, and the amenities and facilities, including the vast employmet opportunities provided, clearly demonstrate that sincere efforts had been put in to create a climate favourable to shifting and whatever little grievance the resettled family had would have been removed speedily, as was our experience with other squatters. Unfortunately, due to the extraneous factor of family planning and incitement and consequent disturbance and police action, the excellent rapport and understanding, which the DDA was able to establish generally with the resettled families, could not straight-away be established in this case. Thereafter, some outside elements came in and complicated the issue.

In such operations, there may be genuine teething trouble,

but the overall advantage which accrue from resettlement in the new site become clear to the allottees in due course. I am sure, this would have happened in this case as well.

Factors that Caused the Incident on 19 April 1976

The DDA carried out clearance-cum-resettlement operations on a very large scale. Because of the considerations shown in resettlement schemes and the incentives and inducements provided and the confidence that was generated by the speed with which development work was done in the new resettlement colonies, there was no incident, not even the slightest gesture of violence or resentment anywhere. About seven lakhs people were resettled and nothing happened anywhere, either before the Turkman Gate incident or afterwards.

Why the Turkman Gate area was the solitary exception? This was because of an extraneous factor—family planning drive launched in the neighbouring localities through Dujana House camp. The campaign was launched on 14-15 April 1976. It created an emotional reaction, particularly in the minority community. This, coupled with incitement and rumours, culminated in the incident of 19 April 1976.

In all the reports of the CID (Special Branch) from 13-14 April to 19-20 April 1976, there was not even the remotest suggestion about any resentment against the demolition/clearance work of DDA in the Turkman Gate area. On the other hand, the reports during this period were full of warnings about the tension that was being built up due to the sterilization drive and rumours spread by vested interests.

In the report of 13-14 April 1976, under the heading "Indian Union Muslims League" the following extract appeared:

> Iqbal Ahmed, Secretary, Delhi Unit of the Muslims League, Shahiruddin Ashrafi and Abdul Khan are reported to have met in the Delhi Muslim League office on 13.4.1976 and decided to instruct selected League workers to spread rumours in areas of Muslim population alleging death of certain persons due to sterilization.

In report No. 81/76, dated 14-15 April 1976, under the heading "Jamat-e-Islami" the following paragraph appeared:

> Awil Ul Jafar, Mohd. Amin Azmi, Mohd. Rafiq, Faras-at Huss Mohd. Ahasan, Mohd. Shafi Monis, Amir Halqa UP and Dr Nizatullah Siddiqui (Aligarh) Member Majlis-e-Shera of JEI met Mohd. Yousuf, Amir JEI, on April 14 in Tis Hazari Courts. During the course of talks, Mohd. Shafi Monis informed the Amir that he had met the Ibrahim Sulaiman Sait, President IUML a week ago and had requested him to use his good offices for exemption of Muslims from forced sterilization, as ML was the only party which could take up the Muslims' cause at the present juncture....

In report No. 82/76, dated 15-16 April 1976, the following paragraph appeared:

> Syed Abdullah Bukhari, Imam Jama Masjid, while addressing a Friday congregation (about 3,000) today (April 16) said that the people will be soon asked to keep their mouths absolutely shut. He alleged that beggers, physically handicapped persons and pavement vendors, were being subjected to forcible sterilizations.

Again from report No. 83/76, dated 16-17 April 1976, the following extracts may be quoted:

> (b) Ibrahim Sulaiman Sait, President, IUML, visited the Party office Urdu Bazar Jama Masjid on 16.4.76 (evening) when he was apprised by Iqbal Ahmed, Abdul Ahmed, Suleman Saliq and Shahir-ud-Din Ashrafi of Imam Abdullah Bukhari's Friday speech particularly on the issue of sterilization of Muslims.

Another extract from the same report under "Indian Union Muslim League" is as follows:

> It has been reliably learnt that Shahi-u-Din Ashrafi (an active ML worker) met Ibrahim Sulaiman Sait on April 17, and reportedly suggested that ML workers should court arrests

against the Government's campaign for alleged forcible sterilization.

(e) There was some commotion in Matia Mahal, near Dujana House Family Planning Camp, on April 18, 1976 when some hot words were exchanged between one Idris and his supporters on one side and the protagonist of family planning on the other. Tension mounted in the area when some stones were reportedly thrown over a family planning van.

In report No. 85/76, dated 19-20 April 1976, the following paragraph appeared under the heading "Muslim Organisations—Muslims Personal Law Board":

(a) According to a usually reliable source, Majlis-e-Amla of Muslim Personal Law Board met at Delhi on April 18, 1976. During discussions, Ibrahim Sulaiman Sait and Yousuf Patel criticised the Government for allegedly resorting to forcible sterilization and said that such action amounted to interference in the religious affairs of Muslims. The MPL Board passed a resolution criticising "forcible" sterilization as inhuman. . . .

The above reports of the Special Branch of the CID were made in the normal course of work and there was no reason as to why they should be favourable or unfavourable to either of the two organizations of the government—the DDA or the family planning department. These reports made before the incident must be taken as fair, objective and reliable for asessing the cause of the riots. Reporting subsequent to the incident of 19 April 1976 could be biased and attempts could be made to throw the blame, wholly or partly, on the DDA or some other agency. These reports are crucial to the issue of determination of the cause of riots.

The riot first started in Dujana House camp on the morning of 19 April 1976. This would be evident from the police wireless messages. Hartal was also organized and emotions worked up on the issue of compulsory sterilization. The rioters in Turkman Gate area came from outside and a large number of people joined the crowd to express their resentment and annoyance against the family planning drive. The Turkman Gate area, being comparatively open, became the site of the incident. The daily summary report of the CID for 19 April 1976 also supports the view that the disturbances on 19 April 1976 were caused by persons from other areas.

Six persons died in the incident and their particulars are as follows:

1. Salaudin s/o Mohd. Din r/o 1942, Kucha Chelan Delhi.
2. Mohd. Shahid s/o Mohd. Yazin r/o 1674, Suiwalan, Delhi.
3. Mohd. Arif s/o Mohd. Bashir r/o 2393, Kucha Mir Hashim, Delhi.
4. Sagir Ahmed Amir s/o Majid Ahmed r/o 3989, Gali Khane Khana, Jama Masjid, Delhi.
5. Om Parkash Omi s/o Meeru r/o 3870, Khirke Tafazal Hussain, Jama Masjid, Delhi.
6. Abdul Malik s/o Abdul Hag r/o 2406, Turkman Gate, Delhi.

This shows that, except for one person who came from Turkman Gate area and whose property was not affected by clearance drive, all other were outsiders from Suiwalan and Jama Masjid area, which is at a distance of about one or two miles from the site.

On 20 April 1976, Mir Mushtaq Ahmed, Chairman, Delhi Metropolitan Council, made a public statement which, inter alia, stated:

There was an incident yesterday in the Turkman Gate area where some anti-social elements tried to obstruct the demolition work which was in progress since 14th April as a part of the redevelopment of the Delhi Ajmeri Gate Improvement Scheme. This was an old scheme, according to which compensation has already been paid in 1940 to the residents. Part of the area was cleared last year and alternative accommodation was provided.

Yesterday in the afternoon certain elements of the Muslim Leage and the banned organization—Jamaite Islami—instigated the undesirable elements of the area to launch an unprovoked attack on the demolition staff and police. They were also provoked by the Imam of Jama Masjid who visited the area earlier in the day.

The Additional District Magistrate's report, made on 19 April 1976 evening, also indicates that family planning drive and incitement by certain interests were the dominant reasons for the incident. It reads, inter alia, as under:

> Earlier in the morning Imam Jama Masjid rang up ADM Central Ashok Pradhan and S.H. Naqvi, A.D.M. (s) and alleged that in the family planning camp being run at Dujana House forcible sterilizations were being carried out and that there was lot of resentment amongst the Muslims of the area against the use of coercive methods. He also threatened to personally lead a group of men and women and offer arrests against the alleged high-handedness in the family planning campaign. The Imam made a speech at about 9.30 A.M. against the family planning in the Jama Masjid area from the P.A. system installed in the mosque. Shortly thereafter at about 9.50 A.M. a car carrying a doctor to the family planning camp at Dujana House was stopped in Bazar Matia by some miscreants, the driver was beaten up and the doctor assaulted. The atmosphere became tense and the Bazar was closed down. A number of women assembled there made a vain bid to mob the organisers of the camp, shouting slogans. The Imam himself came to the family planning camp at Dujana House at about 10.45 A.M. and tried to incite the crowd mainly consisting of women.

In his deposition at the "assistant stage" Ashok Pradhan also disclosed the following facts:

> ....the first incident was at Dujana House.... Actually, if Imam Sahib had not come to the spot [Dujana House] that day and he had not gone to the Turkman Gate area, the things would not have gone beyond control as it happened later.... I told Imam Sahib that I was appealing to him as a man and not as ADM and would request that he should leave the spot [Dujana House] otherwise there will be bloodshed....
> But by the time, I could handle the situation at Dujana

House itself Imam Sahib had left for Turkman Gate. Imam Sahib was opposed to it [family planning] and in the morning he had rung me up on the telephone and told me that if they did not stop he would himself lead women folk and court arrest in protest thereof. . . .

This again shows that the riots occurred due to strong resistance to the family planning programme and incitement of Imam Sahib, and not due to the clearance operation of the DDA. This was also confirmed by R.K. Ohri, Superintendent of Police, who stated in his deposition before the Commission that Saxena, SDPO, had told him that there was resentment against family planning, and not against demolition. K.S. Bajwa, former SP (CID), also stated that there was no intelligence report with him before 19 April 1976, indicating any resentment due to the clearance operation in Turkman Gate area.

It is significant to note that reference to any resentment due to demolition operation appears in the official report for the first time only after the incident had taken place. Before the incident there was no such reference. Nor was there any warning or advice to me by the CID or local Police Station or Superintendent of Police of the area concerned or the district authorities or any other agency or department.

So far as the DDA was concerned, the operation was moving smoothly and steadily, without any indication of resentment or grievances. The strength of the additional police deployed was not significant. There were only three Sub-Inspectors on 13 April 1976, one Inspector and two Sub-Inspectors on 14 April 1976, one Sub-Inspactor and one Inspector on 15 April 1976, one Inspector and one Sub-Inspector on 16 April 1976, one Inspector and two Sub-Inspectors on 17 April 1976. This was obviously not the strength which suggests any likelihood of violence or trouble. The operation, in fact, was so smooth that the necessity of keeping a full contingent of DSP (Demolition Squad) was not felt by the clearance party from 13 to 19 April 1976. A part of the demolition squad was deployed elsewhere.

On 18 April 1976, being Sunday, the clearance party of the DDA did not come to the site, but a very small bulldozer continued to work, clearing the debris by the roadside. If the persons affected with the clearance operation had been really angry with the DDA, they could have certainly attacked the unescorted bulldozer which was functioning with a lone driver without the assistance of any member of the clearance party.

On the morning of 19 April 1976, the DDA staff at the site suspended this operation after noticing certain developments. If the cause of resentment had been the operation of the DDA, the crowd would have been satisfied. But the real cause was different—emotional reaction to the sterilization drive and the speeches made by the leaders of the community on this drive. In this connection, it is significant to note that the Lieutenant Governor had issued a public statement warning that those who opposed the family planning campaign would be severely dealt with.

It is thus quite clear that the Deputy Commissioner, other district officers of the police and magistracy, the Inspector General of Police and the Lieutenant Governor had full information about the strong resentment that was being built all over the walled city against the family planning drive, and yet no steps were taken to relieve the tension. On the contrary, public warnings were given by the Lieutenant Governor to the opponents of the family planning on 10 April 1976 and 15 April 1976. While inaugurating the family planning camp at Dujana House on 15 April 1976, the Lieutenant Governor warned that the Delhi Administration would not tolerate any opposition to the family planning.

If DDA's action was unpopular or there was any resentment because of it, why a simple letter or note could not be sent to me by the Inspector General of Police or any of his staff, the District Magistrate or the Additional District Magistrate, the Chief Secretary or the Home Secretary, Lieutenant Governor or his staff, etc. If anyone had written to the DDA, advising suspension or stoppage of clearance operations, and if the DDA had not acted on the advice or started arguments about it, the blame could be passed on to it. In the long history of its clearance-cum-resettlement drive, not in a single case the DDA has taken action against the advice of the police or magistracy. All sorts of oral statements, unsupported by written communications, even in cases where such communications must be sent, have been made before the Commission to escape responsibilities and unfairly blame others.

After the incident of 19 April 1976, it was the family planning camp at Dujana House that was ordered to be closed by the Lieutenant Governor and no suspension or termination of clearance operation was ordered. If he had felt that the disturbances were due to clearance operation he would have certainly got it stopped. The authorities knew the real cause. Kishan Chand and Mohsin, Deputy Minister (Home), visited the site after 19 April and neither of them ordered stoppage of clearance operation.

So far as the clearance operation in Turkman Gate area was concerned, it could not have led to resentment because the conditions of living in this area were extremely hazardous, and liberal treatment was accorded by the DDA in matter of allotment of alternative flats and plots and allotment was made even to those who were not entitled to any accommodation under the earlier approved scheme of the Corporation. Even the latest arrival of squatter got alternative accommodation and commercial allotments were also made liberally. The extent of liberal treatment can be seen from the fact that 28 plots were allotted against property No. 1920/IX; 22 plots against 3299/VIII; 19 plots against 3271/VIII; 14 plots against 3333/VIII; and 22 plots against 3375/VIII. The two mosques in the area, which had been badly damaged due to the unauthorized constructions on the walls, etc., were specially renovated by the DDA at a cost of Rs 80,000. This was specially appreciated by the Muslim community, and this fact was mentioned in the report of the Special Branch (CID). Subsequently, an additional piece of land was also leased to one of the mosques for its use. Incidentally, this also indicates that there was no communal bias in the approach of the DDA.

DEPLOYMENT OF POLICE

It has already been explained that clearance in the cases of slums and squatter settlements is resorted to through incentives, which make the process of clearance-cum-resettlement smooth, and capable of being completed within a short span, thereby curtailing the period of uncertainty and temporary difficulties inherent in shifting from one place to another. The deployment of police and magistracy in such operations is usual. There are standing instructions of the Lieutenant Governor on the subject. These instructions, issued vide order No. F. 50(6)/67-L&B, dated 27 July 1967, read, inter alia, as under:

> In the recent past a few major demolition-cum-clearance operation have been undertaken and many more have to be carried out in the near future. The problems connected with the operations are very complicated. A political slant is now sought to be given to every operation and strong resistance is being put up by vested interests. It is, therefore, absolutely necessary to strengthen the demolition-cum-clearance machinery and to make available its assistance to all the departments concerned.
>
> All the Heads of Departments of Delhi Administration are directed to give the fullest cooperation and assistance to the [Demolition] Cell and attend to the requirements of the [Demolition] Cell on a high priority basis. Whenever any major operation has to be undertaken at least the S.D.M., D.S.P. of the local area would remain with the demolition party throughout the operation.

It was in accordance with these instructions and the usual practice that communication No. PA/VC/76/Dem., dated 7 April 1976, asking for deployment of police, was sent by me to the DIG, with a copy to the District Magistrate and other concerned. This letter was written after discussions with the Lieutenant Governor on 5 April 1976 and taking his approval to the line of action contemplated.

A copy of the above letter to the DIG was sent through special messenger to the District Magistrate, three Superintendents of Police concerned, DSP (Demolition Squad), Secretary to the Lieutenant Governor and other concerned. Except the SP (Central) who wanted the date to be changed and this was agreed to, concurrence of all concerned was evident. No one indicated any difficulty or raised any objection. The DSP (Demolition Squad), DDA also intimated to the SP (Central) that clearance would be taken up in Turkman Gate area and thereafter the Deputy Commissioner (Slums) and the staff were in touch with the police and magistracy which came to the site from 13 April 1976 onwards. The operation commenced on 13

April 1976 and continued peacefully and smoothly on 14 April, 15 April, 16 April, and 17 April 1976. On 18 April 1976, being Sunday, no clearance work was done. Due to reasons stated earlier, disturbances took place on 19 April 1976.

The fact that an endorsement of my letter was made semi-officially to the Secretary to the Lieutenant Governor shows that the matter had been discussed with the Lieutenant Governor; otherwise there would have been no point in making the endorsement. Secondly, when the letter states that the operation to be undertaken is a sensitive one, how could it be treated as unimportant communication, particularly when it was sent through special messenger and marked "Most Immediate"?

In such cases, help of the police force and magistracy is asked for maintenance of law and order, preventing possible physical interference of outside elements and vested interests, controlling general traffic, for securing orderliness in the movement of men and vehicles, and for keeping watch over luggage and other material, etc.

For sensitive or major operation, it is a usual practice to write to the DIG or Deputy Commissioner to make law and order arrangements. Copies of the communications are also sent to all concerned. In this connection, it is relevant to compare the communication sent by me to the DIG with a copy to Deputy Commissioner, on 7 April 1976 with the following three communications sent to the Deputy Commissioner with a copy to the DIG in connection with three clearance operations undertaken before the emergency.

1. F. 50(1)/67-L&B, dated 6/7th March, 1968.
2. F. 50(50)/68-L&B, dt. 7th November, 1968.
3. F. 3(66)/73-CRC/DDA, dated 12th February 1974.

From the above three communications and similar other communications sent from time to time to district and police authorities, with copies to civic authorities and Special Assistant to the Lieutenant Governor, it would be quite clear that the practice of deployment of police and magistracy in the manner it was done in Turkman Gate was in vogue before the emergency and there has been no departure from the practices followed earlier.

Even after the emergency, the practice has not changed. In this connection, I quote from the note of the Executive Officer (Demolition), dated 14 May 1977, which he wrote in connection with the clearance operation in Jafrabad area:

> Clearance operation in Jafrabad, where 3,000 to 4,000 sirkies had come up recently, was undertaken yesterday. Two companies of the armed police were also requisitioned. We had arranged about 125 beldars and labourers.
>
> Since they refused to cooperate, they were detained by the local police. Most of these sirkies were removed by the unauthorised encroachers themselves. In the meantime, about 200-300 women collected around the jail van. The force was collected and brought to the location where 2 companies of the DAP were kept standby by the local police. The unauthorised encroachers indulged in setting fire to their sirkies at about 15-20 locations. This fire was witnessed by ADM(E), DIG(R), SP(E) and all other officers.

There are a number of other cases in which similar procedure has been adopted after April 1977. These cases include demolition in Motia Khan, Subzimandi and Geeta Colony, etc. In the last mentioned colony, a number of persons were arrested.

The request for the presence of police and magistracy for the clearance of site in question, Turkman Gate, was normal and does not mean that forcible eviction was to be secured. If that had been so, much larger police forces should have been called and entire clearance operation finished in a day or so. After all, there were only about 120 houses and one transit camp to be cleared. The very fact that many incentives and inducements were provided and the clearance operation carried out slowly and smoothly and was spread over a long period of time, about 15 days, shows the intention of the DDA. The allottees took their own time in moving out. They removed the doors and window frames, asbestos sheets, took roof ballies and other material, etc. In this connection, it is relevant to quote from the Assistant Engineer's note No. D/88/A.E.II/S-IV/76, dated 19 April 1976, which, inter alia, reads as under:

> It has been seen that before vacating, the occupants remove

all wooden structures such as doors and windows chokats including shutters, wooden battens and other fittings. In some cases it is seen that even dismantling of structures is done by the occupants and they remove karries and stone slabs in process.

This note was written in the normal course of work. The Assistant Engineer noted that the occupants were removing building material from their houses. As the houses were the properties of the DDA, the Assistant Engineer thought that some blame might not come to him for allowing salvageable building material to be taken away by the occupants. This clearly shows that there was no attempt on the part of staff of the Slum Department to hustle through the operation. The occupants were moving slowly and steadily. The average demolition of the structures would come to eight or nine per day.

The contention that force was not used is further supported by the fact that allotment slips were obtained by the occupants of the following properties but no demolition took place as they were not vacated:

3173; 3174; 3179; 3182; 3213; 3220; 3223; 3226; 3227; 3191; 3222; and 3225.

Much has been made of what has been termed as bulldozing operation. The reality, in fact, is different. Bulldozing was done only after the site or building had been vacated. It was merely a labour and time-saving technique, and helped in the speedy clearance of debris and implementation of development projects.

In clearing the pocket of land in question, only one small bulldozer (D4) was deployed from 13 April 1976 to 18 April 1976. It was only after 19 April 1976 that a number of bulldozers were deployed, at the request of the police, to clear the debris as speedily as possible.

On 19 April 1976, when the incident took place, I was in the office attending to some important work. I received a wireless message about 3 P.M. indicating that the police required larger number of bulldozers to be sent to the site immediately. I got in touch with the Engineer Member, DDA, and other staff concerned and replied that it would take some time to arrange additional bulldozers. I understand that the anxiety of the police and magistracy was that the debris should be got cleared as quickly as possible so that stones and other rubbles could not be used by any person wanting to create further trouble. It was also indicated that the area should be floodlit and work carried out on priority basis to complete the removal of debris as speedily as possible.

It was not only in the case of Turkman Gate area but also in numerous other cases that bulldozers were deployed to secure speedy clearance of the debris. This practice of deploying the bulldozers had been in vogue for over a decade. Major clearance operation like that of Yamuna Bazar and Nizamuddin were carried out by deploying bulldozers. If the bulldozers had not been deployed in sufficient strength and for longer time, the rubble would have remained at the site for a number of days.

Late in the evening, on 19 April 1976, I discussed the matter with the Lieutenant Governor. He wanted the clearance operations to continue.

I sent a report to the controlling ministry i.e., the Ministry of Works and Housing, vide my d.o. letter No. PA/VC/76/494, dated 20 April 1976.

The same report was also sent to the Lieutenant Governor, vide my d.o. No PA/VC/76/493, dated 21 April 1976. It was received in his office the same day. The case was also discussed in the ministry on 24 April 1976, and the ministry wanted to know the latest position. I supplied the requisite information vide my d.o. letter No. PA/VC/76/520, dated 26 April 1976.

These reports and communications to the Governor and Secretary, Ministry of Works and Housing, clearly show that no instructions of Lieutenant Governor or the central government, who were fully in picture, had been issued for the suspension or stoppage of the clearance operations and these operations were continuing with their approval.

That the Lieutenant Governor was actively directing and approving such clearance operations is further reinforced by his visit to the Turkman Gate site on 21 April 1976, his talk with H.K. Lal, Deputy Commissioner (Slums), at the spot, and his approval of the clearance operation of Sarai Khaleel area about three weeks after the Turkman Gate clearance.

I may refer to the "daily situation reports" of the ADM from 23 April 1976 onwards, which he started submitting to S.L. Khurana, Home Secretary, in accordance with the latter's directives on the subject.

In her report of 23 April 1976, Mrs Meenakshi Datta Ghosh, ADM, inter alia, stated: "Today it [the DDA's operation] was largely confined to the removal of debris of the demolition carried out earlier. There was no fresh demolition." In her daily situation reports of 24 April 1976, the ADM recorded: "33 vacant houses are being demolished. Persons inhabiting these houses vacated them two days ago after receipt of slips from DDA for alternative house sites. Meanwhile, the clearance of debris by DDA also continues alongwith repair of the two Masjids." The report of 25 April 1976 states: "The DDA operation continues. The action on 33 vacant houses to be demolished has been completed. No fresh demolition took place today. The clearance of debris by DDA and the repairs to the two mosques is continuing."

The submission of these "daily situation reports" also show that there was no decision taken in a meeting called by the Home Secretary to stop demolition or clearance operations after 19 April 1976. The statement of the previous Inspector General of Police, Bhawani Mal, before the Commission that such a decision was taken is, therefore, incorrect. If any such decision had been taken, the Home Secretary would have issued directive to the Lieutenant Governor or written to the Ministry of Works and Housing to instruct the DDA to stop demolition operations.

In this connection, it is also relevant to quote from the notes, dated 22 April 1976, of the Deputy Commissioner and the Chief Secretary. In his note Sushil Kumar, former Deputy Commissioner, observed:

> The present demolition operation of the DDA needs to be stopped. On the other hand, removal of unauthorised occupants on Government land and their re-settlement elsewhere have also to be carried out.

Kohli, Chief Secretary, in his note recorded:

> A decision to stop the demolition work or to proceed with it is by its very nature a very difficult one. In view of its obvious

law and order implications, the Deputy Commissioner has recommended its stoppage. However, the implication of the stoppage in the circumstances might well be that it may not be possible in the immediate future to take up that demolition work again. The choice is between two alternatives, neither of which is totally satisfactory. L.G. may kindly consider whether he would like to call an urgent meeting with VC, DDA, Dy. Commissioner, I.G.P. and myself.

Both the above-quoted notes clearly show that up to 22 April 1976, no decision had been taken to stop the demolition operation. In fact, Kohli, Chief Secretary, had suggested two alternatives. The Lieutenant Governor neither called any meeting nor ordered stoppage of demolition. This clearly shows that the continuance of the operation for a few days after 19 April 1976 was in accordance with the Lieutenant Governor's approval.

The Deputy Commissioner's note of 22 April 1976 states "that it will take DDA not less than three days to complete the present work." In fact, the DDA took not more than three or four days after 22 April 1976. This also clearly shows that the DDA's operation after 19 April 1976 was of a limited nature and mainly confined to removal of rubble, bulldozing the earth, and clearing all vacated structures.

The curfew was imposed by the district authorities and Lieutenant Governor entirely due to different considerations and had nothing to do with the DDA's clearance operation. In fact, the curfew continued for 45 days, and its continuance shows the attitude which the Lieutenant Governor had adopted in the matter. His posture before the Commission totally contradicts the written record. If he had issued any instructions regarding stoppage of demolition operation after 19 April 1976, why could he not send a written letter or a note to the DDA or the district authorities?

PRIVATE PROPERTY?

To the best of my knowledge, there was no private property in the pocket of the land cleared. All the properties had been acquired on the basis of Land Acquisition Notification which had been issued in the Government of India *Gazette* on 19 March

1938, and entire slum clearance scheme was approved by the Chief Commissioner vide his order notified in the *Gazette* of India, dated 4 May 1966.

The position in this regard has, however, been not fully clear, primarily because of the long pendency of the case extending over three to four decades. During this period, it appears, some files were lost or misplaced and the land records were either manipulated by interested parties or acquired properties were not included in the relevant registers due to oversight or clerical error. This difficulty was aggravated by the splitting of original survey numbers into different municipal numbers and further replacement of the old municipal numbers by new municipal numbers. Some decisions of the Delhi Improvement Trust in respect of the abandonment of a few properties in the total area of the scheme on certain terms and conditions added to the difficulties.

Transfer of slum clearance work from the Delhi Improvement Trust/DDA to the Delhi Municipal Corporation in 1960 and its retransfer to the DDA from the Delhi Municipal Corporation caused considerable diffusion of responsibility in regard to maintenance of file and registers. Taking advantage of the position some persons seem to have got their names inserted in the property registers of the Delhi Municipal Corporation.

It appears that at the time of transfer of slum clearance work from the Delhi Improvement Trust/DDA to the Delhi Municipal Corporation, the latter prepared the register of properties either incorrectly or took copies from the records which were incomplete or manipulated. The unreliability of the registers of the Slum Department can be assessed from the fact that it does not contain entries with regard to number of properties which have been even shown as belonging to the Delhi Improvement Trust in the old House Tax record of the local body and in respect of which award files are even now available. The properties which were purchased by the Delhi Improvement Trust/DDA from the Delhi Municipal Corporation and the old Nazul properties in the area in question were also not properly accounted for in the records. Subsequent maps, plans, and agenda notes of the Corporation/DDA are based on these incorrect or incomplete entries in the registers of the Slum Department.

The difficulties of the nature referred above are inherent in the long pendency and neglect of the case. Nevertheless, there is little doubt that all the properties cleared in the clearance operation in the question were public properties. This would be evident from the following:

(*a*) The original land acquisition notification published in 19 March 1938 covers a compact area with no pocket of property left. The schedule and map referred to in this notification make it absolutely clear.

(*b*) In view of the considerations of compact and integrated development and higher standard of development in the area facing Asaf Ali Road, exclusion of any isolated building from the purview of acquisition in the pocket of land cleared was highly unlikely.

(*c*) It was precisely for securing integrated and compact redevelopment of the area that all the evacuee/custodian properties were got transferred by the then Prime Minister from the Ministry of Rehabilitation to the DDA/DMC on cost which would have been payable if the properties in question had been acquired under the provisions of the Slum Areas (Improvement and Clearance) Act, 1956.

(*d*) In the area of Delhi Ajmeri Gate Scheme, 13,454 sq. yds. of land was purchased from the Delhi Municipal Committee by the DIT at a cost of Rs 1.68 lakhs on the basis of the Resolution No. 355, dated 22 August 1938. The lands which accrued to the then Delhi Municipal Committee following the demolition of the city wall were also transferred to the Delhi Improvement Trust for implementation of the Delhi Ajmeri Gate Slum Clearance. Again, 18.79 acres of Nazul (government land) was also transferred to the DIT by the government for the said scheme (reference of this exist in Resolution No. 169, dated 27 May 1952).

(*e*) In 1947, the Delhi Improvement Trust decided to abandon a few properties from acquisition under Section 64-A of the Trust laws which provided "that the owner of a land comprised in an improvement scheme might make an application to the Trust requesting that acquisition of his/her land be abandoned on suitable terms." In respect of abandonment, the Trust laid down the following principles vide its Resolution No. 215, dated 23 October 1947:

(*i*) Any residential area which is under 150 sq. yds. must be acquired. The reason for this is, that an area less than this size (subject to minor marginal adjustment) will have to be regarded as too small for suitable construction.

(*ii*) The remaining plots will be dealt with under two heads:

(*a*) Where the properties standing on the plots are so badly designed or constructed decision will be taken by the Trust in each case on the advise of Health and Engineering experts.

(*b*) Where buildings are not in such an unsatisfactory condition as to be classified as "Slum", demolition will not be insisted upon, except for building standing on that portion of the site, which has got to be handed over to the Trust for execution of their scheme. In the net area thus retained by the owner, he will pay a similar charge per sq. yd. to cover the cost of execution of the scheme.

Subsequently, vide its Resolution No. 109, dated 4 April 1952, it was resolved that abandonment fee-rate should be Rs 40 and Rs 30 per sq. yd for (*a*) and (*b*) class respectively.

From the above, it is clear that any person who claims that his/her land was abandoned from acquisition has to fulfil the following requirements:

(*i*) The applicant must have made a representation to the Improvement Trust for release/abandonment of the property from acquisition, and the Trust must have accepted the representation for release. There must also be a regular release deed in the form annexed with the Resolution No. 157, dated 26 May 1953 of the Trust.

(*ii*) The area of the land/property must be more than 150 sq. yds.

(*iii*) The land/property should qualify for release on the basis of the two conditions laid down in (*a*) and (*b*) as of (*ii*) above.

(*iv*) The owner must have paid the abandonment fee on the rates prescribed by the Trust vide its Resolution No. 109, dated 4 April 1952, i.e. Rs 40 per sq. yd. for (*a*) class and Rs 30 for (*b*) class of properties.

The Trust considered various applications/representations vide its Resolution No. 25, dated 22 January 1953; No. 92, dated 17 March 1953, No. 157, dated 26 May 1953; and No. 236, dated

4 August 1953. None of the property in the pocket of land in question was agreed to be abandoned by any of these resolutions. (Similar was the position with regard to the properties scheduled for improvement. No improvement fee was paid by anyone and no exclusion from acquisition took place.)

(f) Because of the incomplete records, little doubt had crept in and the field staff checked up the position from the occupants. Not a single person or occupant made any claim about ownership or produced any ownership document with regard to any of the properties of the area not included in the list of the register of the Slum Department. Nor could the occupants of the building produce any rent receipt in favour of any landlord. No worthwhile claim of ownership was put in to any authority even after clearance and resettlement of the occupiers in the DDA colonies had been carried out.

(g) Notwithstanding all that has been stated above, it was decided at the time of clearance that, because of the long pendency of the case and neglect of records, if someone came with a reliable evidence to show that a particular property belonged to him and Deputy Commissioner (Slums) was satisfied in this regard, due compensation as per provisions of the Slum Areas (Improvement and Clearance) Act, 1956 could be paid to him.

(h) Subsequently in early March 1977, when I heard some allegations in this regard, I asked for a report, and it was reported to me by the Slum Department that only three claims had been received and only one case had some basis in the claim and compensation of about Rs 400 had been assessed in respect of that claim.

From the above facts, it is reasonably clear that the properties cleared in the clearance operation were public properties and whatever little doubt existed was cleared and dealt with in a bonafide manner. No advantage can be taken by anyone merely because a particular register is incomplete or has been manipulated.

In any case, no instruction whatsoever had been issued by me that any private property should be cleared. The occupants were interested in getting alternative plots which were being allotted on a liberal scale. For instance, 28 plots were allotted against property No. 1920/IX and 22 plots against property

No. 3299/VIII. No question about rent or damage or any connected issue was asked. They themselves removed the *karies* and other salvageable building material before taking the truck to the new site. If LIG/MIG flats were asked for, they were also allotted as a measure of incentive.

At worst, what can be said is that there are five properties in which acquisition by the Delhi Improvement Trust cannot be established on the basis of the award papers and references pertaining to the thirties and forties, but in respect of which there is sufficient circumstantial evidence (Improvement Trust resolutions quoted above) to prove that these properties had not been excluded from the purview of acquisition. The number of such properties is not twenty-nine, as is being given out. The original municipal number of properties (five) has been split up into twenty-nine, as over the years, rooms of the same unit were partitioned by insubstantial walls or tin sheds. Even in respect of five doubtful cases, the total amount of compensation payable would not have exceeded Rs 10,000. Being notified slums, compensation would have been calculated on the basis of sixty months rental value, minus 40 per cent.

The so-called private properties have no "private owners." This would be evident from the following press advertisement issued by the post-emergency administration on 21 March 1978:

> In April 1976 some buildings in Turkman Gate area (Ward VIII) were demolished by the Delhi Development Authority. While most of these buildings had been acquired long back under the Delhi Ajmeri Gate Scheme, it is suspected that some of these buildings could be private property. All the persons, who claim ownership of any property which was demolished in this area in April 1976, are requested to submit their claims alongwith supporting documents to Assistant Commissioner (Slums), Delhi Development Authority, Jhandewalan Extension, New Delhi 110055 by the 31st March 1978.

Even one year after the emergency, the present authorities were not sure of the position of "private properties." They had mere suspicions. Significantly, the aforesaid press advertisement was issued after my evidence at the "assistance-stage" had been recorded, and my line of defence had become known.

Our bonafide would be clear from the fact that instructions had been issued by me in April 1976 that, because of the cases being thirty or forty years old, benefit of doubt should be given to the persons who claimed ownership and produced worthwhile, if not conclusive, evidence. In the two doubtful cases, namely of Islam-uddin and Ibrahim, properties were cleared only after their written consent was given. Both of them obtained DDA middle income group flats. Eight other witnesses deposed before the Commission about the properties with which they were connected. None of them is the owner. This would be evident from the particular of the properties given in Appendix III. In fact, boot is on the other leg. The occupants used public properties for a number of years, and in some cases took rent from others. To cap it all, they obtained a large number of alternative plots and flats against properties which had been notified as slum about forty years ago, and which were dangerous and dilapidated. For instance, against nine properties referred to in Appendix III, 105 alternative plots and flats were obtained. Besides Ibrahim, who gave his consent in writing and obtained middle-income group flat from the DDA, not a single person came before the Commission and said, "I am the owner of property No. 'A' and here is my ownership document." Is it not worth pondering that, notwithstanding all the publicity and the efforts of investigating agencies and Fact Finding Committee, and inducement of securing compensation, such persons could not be produced. The reality is that there were no owners. A few persons were merely taking advantage of incorrect or manipulated entries in the Municipal and DDA records, and some factually incorrect notes were prepared on the basis of the inaccurate entries. Such inaccuracies are bound to occur when a case remains pending for over thirty or forty years. In any case, there were only a couple of persons with doubtful claims. Against this background, imagine the allegation that thousands of houses were demolished by the DDA!

CONTEMPLATED CHANGE OF LAND

Huge funds are required for the Slum Clearance and Improvement Scheme. For instance, in Delhi, in addition to the funds required for resettlement of squatters occupying lands needed for public purposes, about 425[4] crores are required to build tenements for 2,74,000[5] families living in notified slums. An idea of the requirement of the funds and the funds actually available can be formed from the fact that only Rs 60 crores were made available by the central government for the entire country during the period from the commencement of the five-year plans to 1971.

In view of this, suggestions have been made from time to time to augment resources by using a portion of the slum land for commercial purposes. Two such suggestions may be cited here:

(a) Soon after the transfer of the slum work to the DDA, a meeting[6] was held in the Ministry of Works and Housing on 18 May 1974. It was decided that the DDA might draw composite scheme of slum clearance, containing commercial components, so that subsidy element could be reduced and the scheme made self-financing to a considerable extent.

(b) In another meeting held in the room of Minister of State for Works and Housing on 18 September 1974, Baleshwar Prasad, the then Lieutenant Governor, observed that the schemes were held up as the estimated cost of tenements exceeded the prescribed ceiling. It was felt that some remunerative project should be taken up to meet the financial constraints.

It was in the context of the above thinking that it was decided to explore the possibility of using the cleared land for commercial purposes. This pocket was considered specially suitable for commercialization for the following reasons:

(a) Modern commercial complexes had been developed on both sides of the pocket.

(b) The locational advantage for commercialization was enhanced by the existence of the road connecting Asaf Ali Road with Jawaharlal Nehru Marg and the proposed construction of school and bridge connecting Jawaharlal Nehru Marg with Barakhamba Road over the railway lines in accordance with the provisions of the Master Plan.

(c) The location of the pocket was such that pressure for commercialization would mount. Even if the land was used for residential purposes, it was likely to be converted for commercial purposes by the allottees.

(d) There was a large number of non-conforming office and commercial establishments inside the congested area of the city and these offices and commercial establishments could be pursuaded to move out of the small bazars into the new commercial complex that could be developed on the pocket of land in question, thereby serving the twin purpose of raising additional funds and decongesting the interior portion of the city and eliminating the movement of the vehicles in the narrow lanes and by-lanes.

But the extent and the manner in which commercialization of the pocket could be carried out depended on the soil investigation and test bores which could be effectively undertaken after the clearance of the site. Height of the building, floor-area ratio, and provision of parking space in the basement would also depend on the result of the surveys and investigations.

Immediately after the clearance, the Chief Engineer of the DDA wrote to the Central Design Organization of the CPWD on 4 May 1976 to conduct soil investigations tests and dig four test bores and communicate the results. As soon as the results of the investigations were available, the Town Planner formulated his proposal. As these proposals envisaged commercialization of the area with FAR 400, it was required to be put up to the DDA and central government for approval. Accordingly, an agenda note was prepared and put up to the DDA in its meeting held on 30 July 1976. This agenda note, inter alia, read as under:

While studying the problems of Walled City, it is found that residential population of the area has decreased from 4.20 lakhs in 1961 to 4.11 lakhs in 1971 but on the other hand, volume of commercial activities has increased as given below:

Sl. No.	Business Types	No. of units in 1961	1972	Percentage growth over 1961
1.	Shops	22,474	41,984	86.81
2.	Commercial establishments	38,581	85,736	122.22
3.	Restaurants	980	2,920	197.00
	Total	62,035	1,30,640	110.59

To reduce congestion from the Walled City, it is proposed to use this pocket for General Business and Commerce with a FAR of 400.

In the meeting held on 30 July 1976, presided over by the Lieutenant Governor/Chairman, DDA, the DDA considered this agenda note and passed the following resolution:

Resolved that the proposals contained in the agenda item be approved and follow-up action for change of land use initiated in accordance with the provisions of the Delhi Development Act, 1957.

When the above resolution came up for confirmation in the next meeting of the DDA on 4 September 1976 a member raised certain points. After discussions, it was resolved that the matter should be left over to the Lieutenant Governor/Chairman, DDA for decision. Subsequently, the Lieutenant Governor considered the matter and decided on 12 October 1976 that the original resolution passed by the DDA in its meeting held on 30 July 1976 should stand. The matter was referred to the central government which approved the proposal, in terms of the Delhi Development Act. Thereafter, the proposed changes were notified for inviting public objections. By the time the public objections were received and considered, the new government had taken over. In view of the revised thinking on the subject, the DDA/central government dropped the proposal of making changes in the land-use and FAR, etc.

GENERAL

The problems of Shahjahanabad, the walled city, with some of its localities having the highest congestion rate in the world, are so acute that they can be solved only through a fundamental approach. In my articles published in the *Hindustan Times* in 1974 and my book *Rebuilding Shahjahanabad*, I had made a number of suggestions to reorganize and rejuvenate life in this old and historic city. One of the suggestions was setting up of a new settlement, Second Shahjahanabad, in Minto-Mata-Sundari

Road Complex, the area lying between Ramlila Ground and New Delhi. I had advocated:

> Such a settlement is absolutely necessary not only for restoring the organic entity of the total city but also for rejuvenating Shahjahanabad. It could, on the one hand, absorb smoothly and speedily the surplus population of Shahjahanabad while, on the other, it could emerge as a new centre of social and cultural stimulation from which the ripples of change might seep into the stagnant fabric of the walled city.
>
> So far, modern Indian settlements have either been the products of Western thinking, or they have been allowed to emerge, without any control or direction, out of poverty, degradation and indifference. What is needed is a conscious and creative effort to evolve a settlement which is true to the soil, which respects our healthy traditions, and which represent new needs and aspirations. The Second Shahjahanabad gives an opportunity to create such a settlement. Will we rise to the occasion, or allow another odd colony to develop between old Shahjahanabad and New Delhi?

The above suggestion was endorsed by a high-level seminar (February 1975) organized at the initiative of the then Prime Minister Indira Gandhi. The recommendations of the seminar were accepted by the central government. This, inter alia, implied reservation of the entire land in the Minto-Mata Sundari Road Complex for absorption of old and surplus population of the walled city in Second Shahjahanabad and relocation of squatters in the trans-Yamuna area.

After acceptance of the proposal, however, no action was allowed to be taken by certain vested interests, and the project of Second Shahjahanabad has been shelved. Yet, it is not those who frustrated the project who are being blamed; it is those who wanted to provide real and lasting relief to half a million people jampacked into a choking, stuffy and stinking slum that is now Shahjahanabad.

In any case, the inhuman slum of Turkman Gate comprising mostly dangerous and dilapidated buildings had to go. Its removal before the rainy season of 1976 eliminated the risk of house collapses and consequent loss of life.

Conclusion

What does this untold story of Turkman Gate indicate? Was it arbitrary to implement a scheme which was sanctioned by the Improvement Trust and the Corporation years ago, and clear the dangerous and dilapidated houses and thus save the occupants from the risk of death? Where are thousands of "owners" whose thousands of houses were demolished? How is it that not a single person (except Ibrahim who gave his consent in writing and obtained middle-income-group flat from the DDA), notwithstanding all the adverse publicity and month-long efforts of investigating agencies and fact finding committees and inducement of compensation, came forward and said, "I am the owner of Property 'A' and here is my ownership document." Where are the names and addresses of women and children who are supposed to have been crushed under the bulldozers? Is it not clear that the incident of 19 April 1976 was due to incitement and rumours connected with the family planning campaign? How is it that none of the six persons who died as a result of police firing was affected by the clearance of slum properties and five of them came from distant localities? Is it not ironical that those who passed the Corporation resolution denying allotment to squatters are now denouncing those who implemented the resolution after liberalizing it? And who are the crafty inventors of stories like those of Ranjit Hotel where Sanjay Gandhi, two unidentified women, and myself are supposed to have enjoyed the scene of demolition?

I ask all those who are talking of new values and truth to ponder over these questions and also remember what Gandhiji once said: "Politics bereft of principles are like death traps; they kill the soul of the nation."

CHAPTER IX

NINTH DELHI

> In heaven, there is laid up a pattern of Ideal City which he who desires may behold, and beholding may set his own house in order. Whether such a city now exists, or will ever exist, does not matter. The good man will always live after the manner of this ideal city, having nothing to do with any other.
>
> SOCRATES

What is it that makes the city the most imposing creation of man, the craddle of human civilization, the spiritual workshop of the nation? What forces, what urges, constitute the city, and give distinctive shape and colour to it?

In tracing the origin and growth of the city, it would be a mistake to look to the economic causes alone and ignore fundamental urges of man—his social disposition and religious aspirations. "Before the city was the hamlet and the shrine and the village; and before all that, there was disposition to social life." When the cities were first founded, an old Egyptian scribe tells us, the mission of the founder was to "put the gods in their shrines." These basic social and religious urges played no less significant role than the economic forces in giving shape to the urban form. In fact, the city is an expression of man's mind, and all the attributes of his personality—economic, social, political and cultural. As an economic entity, it is a seat of business and industry; as a social organization, it is a creator of community and collective action; as a political unit, it is a centre of power and government; and as a cultural force, it is a repository of old traditions, a fountainhead of new ideas, an instrument of intellectual advancement, and a moulder of attitudes and thoughts. The all-pervasive character of the city was aptly brought out by Spengler when he in *The Decline of the West* observed: "World history is the history of civic man. Peoples, states, politics, all arts and all sciences rest upon one prime phenomenon of human being, the **town.**"

Perspective

Looking at the city in historical perspective Professor Galbraith recently classified the cities into five main categories: the political household; the merchant city; the industrial city; the camp; and the polyglot metropolis.

Under the first category come the cities which were established as "extensions of the rulers' dwellings" and reflected their imperial will and sense of grandeur. Akbar's Fatehpur Sikri, described by Gascoigne as "the world's most perfectly preserved ghost town," is a telling example of this category. Such cities may be the monuments of the past despotism, but their cultural and architectural heritage has innate attraction of its own. The second category is the merchant city, the trading centre, and the third, "the most loathsome of all," the industrial city. The fourth category, the camp, the suburbia, is the result of flight from the industrial city. The combination of the industrial city and the camp, coupled with comparatively cleaner methods of production and stratification of classes, has produced the fifth category, that is, the post-industrial city or polyglot metropolis.

Delhi is, perhaps, one of the few cities, which reflects, in concentrated form, the characteristics of all the above five categories. Its historicity speaks through its magnificent monuments of medieval and Mughal times, and its colonial past finds expression in its vast boulevards and stately buildings of New Delhi. The *katras* and bazaars of Shahjahanabad have the attributes of a mercantile city, while the worst features of the industrial city are found in the existence of noxious industries right underneath the residential houses and in the flow of toxic wastes and sewage in Najafgarh drain and the Yamuna. The civil lines and the newly constructed farm houses near Mehrauli are the "camps" of our city, and proliferation of the managerial and professional classes, coupled with the new awareness of replacing "foul processes of production with relatively pure ones," impart it the colour of a polyglot metropolis.

Combination of all these factors makes Delhi a unique city, a confluence of old traditions and new forces. Jawaharlal Nehru aptly remarked, "We face the good and bad of India in Delhi city which has been the grave of many empires and the nursery of a republic. What a tremendous story is here; the tradition of millennia of our history surrounds us at every step, and the procession of innumerable generations passes before our eyes."

There is sufficient evidence to suggest that Delhi is one of the oldest cities of the world. The Pandavas, the heroes of the Mahabharata, are believed to have founded a city by the name of Inderprastha or Inderpat at the site which is now covered by Purana Quila and Humayun's tomb. Recent archaeological excavation in the Purana Quila and the discovery in 1966 of rock-edict, an inscription of Asoka (273-36 B.C.) engraved on a rugged rock, near Srinivaspuri, west of Kalkaji temple, leave little doubt about its origins. Its present name is, however, associated with Raja Dillu of Mauryan dynasty who built a city in the first century B.C. near the present settlement of Mehrauli. Over the years, "Dillu" came to be spoken as Dehli or Dilli.

Leaving aside the ancient settlement, Delhi had six distinct cities: Lalkot; Siri; Tughlakabad; Jahan Panah; Ferozabad; and Purana Quila. Shahjahanabad, the city founded by Mughal Emperor, Shahjahan in 1638 on the bank of the Yamuna near the old ruins of Ferozabad, is the seventh city. It is against this background that some historians speak of seven cities of Delhi. The above six cities are now extinct. Only their ruins remain as mute testimony to their past. But Shahjahanabad, the seventh city, is still a living city, accommodating about half a million people in an area of two square miles, nursing in its lanes and bye-lanes the tradition and heritage of about 340 years, and also displaying some of the worst features of decay and decadence, of superficiality and hypocrisy, of chaos and confusion, and of what Katherine Mayo called "materialism turned spiritualism."

Lutyen's New Delhi may be termed as the eighth Delhi. The British rulers were dazzled by the imperial tradition of the city. In December 1911, at the Coronation Durbar, King George V announced the decision to shift the capital from Calcutta to Delhi.

The original site chosen was on the north of the northern ridge, and even the foundation stone was laid. But the Town Planning Commission, comprising G.S.C. Swinton, Edwin

Lutyen and J.A. Brodie, considered the original site unsuitable. On its recommendation the location of the new capital was changed to the area around Raisina Hill. The foundation stone, laid so solemnly, was quietly picked up at midnight by a young Punjabi contractor, Shobha Singh, and taken on a bullock cart, wrapped in a gunny bag, to Raisina hill.

Planning and construction of the new capital was mainly in the hands of Lutyen, an ambitious architect, who in his childhood had dreamt of constructing monumental buildings. "As Faith wills, Fate fulfils." This is what Lutyen in his youth had inscribed upon a casket presented to his would be wife. In his case, fate could not have fulfilled better what his faith had willed. He got the rare opportunity of building a new city, an "Anglo-Indian Rome," which would reflect the might, glory and vastness of the British Empire upon which the sun never set.

The story of the construction of New Delhi is fascinating. In this story come alive strong personalities of planners, builders, and administrators. But the story cannot be told here. I would, however, refer briefly to two episodes which are both interesting and instructive.

Swinton, Lutyen, and Brodie often went on an elephant to survey the site. Once, near the ridge, they entered into an argument about the cost of tunnelling at a point where the ridge was low. So fierce became the argument that Brodie refused to share the same elephant. He "slid off the elephant, walked five miles home with temperature nearing 117 in the shade." Such was his emotional involvement in the project.

Lutyen was keen to build on a grand scale. The cost of his projects mounted. Lord Hardinge, Viceroy, started curtailing his proposals. Lutyen was upset. He ruefully remarked, "Viceroy thinks only of what the place would look like in three years' time: 300 years is what I think of." But Lutyen was not a man to give up easily. He cultivated Lady Hardinge and got his schemes sanctioned through her influence. Once, however, she too got annoyed with Lutyen for side-tracking her suggestion. He employed humour where other skills failed. In an assumed posture of penitence, he told Lady Hardinge: "I will wash your feet with my tears and dry them with my hair. It is true that I have very little hair, but you have very little feet." Lady Hardinge burst into laughter. Her annoyance vanished like thin air. Lutyen got his proposals through. His commitment to the monumentality of his projects was so deep that he employed every method to secure their acceptance.

The above two episodes demonstrate that no great city can be built without the active involvement and support of the top executive authority. A more recent example of the same phenomenon is Chandigarh. But for Nehru's sustained support, Le Corbusier could never have built this dream city. Nor could Baron Haussmann, the City Prefect, from 1853 to 1870, clear the slums of Paris, without encouragement from Napolean III, and lay the vistas and tree lines which have made Paris the most beautiful and exciting city of the world. Great cities are built with the support of great men, with vision and courage, and not by "orphans of the street," constantly hounded by intrigue and selfishness of local factions.

The Delhi master plan, too, made a headway because of Nehru's keen personal interest in the planned development of the city. It was because of his interest and the high esteem in which he held Bhagwan Sahay, the then Chief Commissioner of Delhi, that the latter was able to take up various matters pertaining to the master plan direct with Nehru and secure approval of the union cabinet. Before Bhagwan Sahay's arrival on the scene, the draft master plan was in danger of being lost in the sea of routine, comments, and counter-comments of ministries and departments. After Bhagwan Sahay's transfer, interests of the planned development were well guarded by India's two topmost civil servants—Dharma Vira and Vishwanathan.

Ninth Delhi was beset with formidable problems. It had to deal with some of the most unhealthy features of the five categories of cities discussed above. It had to reckon with the structural legacies of seventh and eighth cities. It had to face the problems of sprawling rehabilitation colonies which were hastily planned and developed in the wake of flux of displaced persons from Pakistan. Added to this were the problems emanating from the flood of migrants and "fall out" of national policies. Over-politicalization of local institutions, emergence of new class of exploiters, with no regard either for the past heritage or future of the city, created numerous other difficulties. Against these negative forces were the positive factors which manifested themselves in the vision of Nehru and his successors and motivation of a few individuals who had both the courage and keenness to explore new horizons.

How new challenges were faced or ignored, how new opportunities were seized or missed, and how some of the most heroic efforts were accompanied by the most treacherous ones constitute the story of Ninth Delhi—its saga of triumph and tragedy, of fulfilment and disappointment. Let us first see the triumphs.

TRIUMPHS

The planning foundation of Ninth Delhi rests on the master plan. But planning in itself would have hardly yielded any results. In India and other developing countries many well-intentioned and well-formulated city planning schemes have been ship-wrecked on the bedrock of implementation. A practical approach, which could meet the challenge of physical, financial and institutional constraints, was called for. Accordingly, simultaneous to the enforcement of the master plan, a scheme of acquisition, development, and disposal of land, with a revolving capital of Rs 5 crores, was formulated and executed. The efforts towards the implementation received a big fillip when, under the inspiration of late Dr A.N. Jha, the DDA set up its own implementation machinery in September 1967. What Ninth Delhi is today is largely the result of sustained development efforts put in by the DDA during the last ten or fifteen years.

Before 1962, the total developed and semideveloped area of urban Delhi was about 40,000 acres. The development effort of Ninth Delhi already covers more than 40,000 acres. In other words, Delhi developed during the last ten or fifteen years is almost equivalent to the entire Delhi developed over the centuries—seventh and eighth combined plus the rehabilitation colonies and other settlements constructed after 1947.

A significant feature of Ninth Delhi was that, notwithstanding legal impediments and extreme paucity of funds at the initial stage, an effective urban land policy was formulated and implemented with the threefold objective of regulating development, ensuring social justice, and raising resources from within the city. All lands falling within the urbanizable limits of the master plan were notified for acquisition. Simultaneously, a "revolving" capital of Rs 5 crores was set up. The programme of acquisition, development and disposal was so designed that about 42,000 acres of land was acquired and the revolving fund of Rs 5 crores resolved to the extent of over 135 crores, that is 27 times its original size.

Element of social justice was successfully introduced. Before the introduction of the scheme, about two-thirds of urban land, suitable for development, had passed into the possession of private parties, many of whom either lacked the financial resources for development and constructing buildings thereon, or whose main motive was speculation, which paid heavy dividents in the context af rapidly rising land values.

After acquisition, lands were leased out in accordance with the needs of different sections of the community and with the stipulation that prescribed land uses would be maintained and buildings constructed within two or three years. No family could secure more than one plot or flat. Resales were restricted under the conditions of lease. In the event of permission for sale being accorded, 50 per cent of the unearned increase had to be paid to the DDA.

A false propaganda by vested interests has created an impression in the public mind that the DDA is selling lands to the rich through public auction. The actual position is entirely different. Leaving aside commercial lands, not more than 1 per cent of the acquired area has been sold through public auction. These auctions, moreover, were restricted to those who have no other residential plot or house in Delhi. A virtual ceiling of 400 sq. yds. was imposed on the size of the plan in 1969. No lay-out plan, with larger sizes of plots, was sanctioned thereafter.

It was because of formulation and implementation of new urban land policy that Ninth Delhi today has large residential colonies, providing accommodation mainly to the poor, low- and middle-income groups. While other cities talked, Ninth Delhi implemented.

The phenomenon of urban squatter is as old as history. Excavation at Ur show that even 8000 years ago, the squatters lived in foul atmosphere. As Toynbee significantly remarked, "There has always been urban proletariat in the swamp beneath the capital of glittering upper works." In Shahjahanabad, too, the congested clusters of the poor were occasionally menaced by disease and fire. Bernier refers to the fire which consumed about 6,000 thatched roots.[1] Consequently, the labourers, artisans and the like could get accommodation only in the already congested areas of Shahjahanabad. It has been calculated that during 1916-1926, when New Delhi was being constructed, there was 28 per cent increase in the population of the walled city and this increase was exclusively confined to the poorer section of the population.[2]

It was in Ninth Delhi that for the first time a conscious attempt was made to treat the squatter as an integral part of the community and provide him not only living space, on secure tenure, and environmental facilities, but also development-oriented avenues of employment and opportunity of acquiring a stable family life. In the earlier chapters, I have already discussed the magnitude of the problem and analyzed the implications of our clearance-cum-resettlement-cum-redevelopment schemes. Suffice here to say, about 2 lakhs residential plots or tenements, covering about 5,000 acres of developed land, were made available to the squatters and slum-dwellers in Ninth Delhi, benefiting a population of 10 lakhs. Most of their colonies and estates, like Naraina and Pandav Nagar, are now in the midst of the city. This, I believe, is a move towards social revolution, a trend which will secure for the urban poor, a greater degree of social justice in the near future.

Those who have not studied the problems in depth are inclined to criticize the standards of development and provision of amenities. This is what world-renowned economist, Barbara Ward, has to say in this regard: "For the great majority of the developing countries, we cannot evade the choice between maintaining present standards and benefits for the few, or designing much more economic minimum standards in order to reach a much wider spectrum of society, and in particular, of course, the urban migrant."

Apart from making available 2 lakhs plots to the poorest of the poor, about 70,000 residential plots, providing acccomodation for 1,40,000 dwelling units, have been developed and allotted in Ninth Delhi either directly or through cooperative housing societies. In addition to plot-housing, group-housing schemes, which aim at constructing simple, inexpensive, functionally utilitarian and aesthetically satisfying houses, have been executed on a large scale. Under these schemes, 38,200 houses had been constructed for Janata, low- and middle-income groups by April 1977. Another 18,000 houses were in different stages of construction, and schemes for construction of yet another 40,000 had been finalized.

Few realize social and economic benefits of large-scale group housing. The individual is saved of the botheration of constructing a house. Simultaneous allotment of flats in large housing estates bring immediate life to the community. Running of bus services, schools and other community facilities become viable. Investment in infrastructure begins to yield full result forthwith.

When a sizeable section of lower and middle income group families were sharing small houses and living in barsaties or garrages, with women and children quarrelling over common latrines, common bathrooms and water taps, not much criticism was seen in the press. Now, when such families are getting independent DDA flats, without undergoing any inconvenience whatsoever, and paying hire-purchase amount, which in most cases works out to be less than the rental value, a lot of criticism appears in the press. Is it not unfortunate? The new housing estates have their teething troubles, but the conditions in them are far better than the places where the allottees were living before.

It will be noticed that Ninth Delhi has, in total, provided residential plots and houses for about 380,000 dwelling units families, i.e. residential need for a population of about 20 lakhs. In April 1977, about half of the families living in Delhi were lessees of the DDA.

One of the basic problems of the metropolitan centres is the tendency to build upon every available open space and to obtain maximum advantage of the high cost of land. Commercial interests dominate. Destruction of natural beauty and landscape seems to be of little consequence to those who are out to make quick profits. Higher human values are ignored. Recreational and cultural needs are relegated to the background. Consequently, the city is reduced to humdrum of brick and mortar, breeding environmental hazards and strangulating human health and happiness.

Ninth Delhi has, however, different planning values. It has

drawn nature into the city. It has ensured that the citizen is able to enjoy, even in the humdrum of urban life, "four ducks on a pond, a green bank beyond." About 25 per cent of the area has been earmarked for green uses, and natural landscape of the ridges, hillocks and river banks maintained.

Ninth Delhi is the only city in the world which has developed in a short time: 49 "mini forests" and woodlands have created humane and delightful environment in harmony with nature; 16 lakhs trees and shrubs have been planted, and about 650 parks and "tot lots" provided. Few realize the tremendous assets created for the future. After visiting some city forests, George Verghese, former editor of the *Hindustan Times*, described them as "landmarks in urban development." G.V. Kaufman, MP, and representative of the British department of environment, wrote: "Congratulations to Delhi on this magnificent concept of providing lungs for its citizens." And this is what D. Peter Jovanovic, Head of the Environment Protection Committee, Yugoslavia, had to say, "I was impressed by the concept of systematic provision of green areas in the broader city tissue of Delhi and by the environmental and economic aspect of parks in the community."

Selection of sites for mini forests, woodlands and parks was made, keeping in view their nearness to historical places. Tughlakabad, Hauz Khas, and Jahan Panah city forests not only provide lungs for the city but also preserve its heritage.

Those who are not familiar with this aspect of development of Ninth Delhi might do well to have a morning walk along the River Front or stroll in the evening in parks around Purana Quila, northern ridge, Kalkaji temple or drive to Dhaula Kuan lake or spend their holidays in Tughlakabad or Hauz Khas city forests. For contrast, they may also see the northern vicinity of Tughlakabad fort, where during the last one year an avalanche of unauthorized construction has descended, butchering green spaces, threatening the architectural legacy of a great monument, and brutalizing the entire landscape. If the sight arouses their civic sense and makes them feel responsible to their children and grandchildren, they may also visit Mayapuri green buffer which for years had been lovingly nursed by us and which now stands punctured by ugly shops and other unauthorized constructions, causing traffic hazards and environmental degradation.

Ninth Delhi has seen rapid emergence of new centres of commercial and institutional activity. A significant feature of the development is that it not only provides for new needs but also helps in decongesting the old city. Non-conforming industries are being shifted from the heart of the city to the newly developed industrial colonies of Naraina, Mayapuri, Wazirpur, Jhilmil, Okhla, etc., which also provide industrial plots. Out of these, about 6,000 plots have already been allotted at fixed price to those industrialists who are required to shift.

Two large shopping and commercial centres, Nehru Place and Rajinder Place, which provide space four times the space available in Connaught Place, have been developed. A new inter-state bus terminus, which can cater to about 1,200 buses at a time, has started functioning. It has removed insufferable traffic congestion near the old Delhi railway station. A new wholesale fruit and vegetable market, Azadpur, a new wholesale cycle market, Jhandewalan, and three new truck terminals have also been set up. The Jama Masjid Complex has been redeveloped and landscaped. The iron merchants' market, Motia Khan, Kabari shop and Lakkar Mandi of Deshbandhu Gupta Road, have been relocated in the newly developed areas of Naraina, Mayapuri, Kirti Nagar, etc.

New mini-subzimandis have been established in Tilak Nagar, Janakpuri, Safdarjang Enclave, Okhla, etc. In addition to these, thousands of new commercial premises have been made available in the shape of built-up shops and plots in various convenient and district shopping centres, such as Basant Lok, Friends Community Centre, Suraj Parbat, etc. Unauthorized dairies have been shifted and relocated in the three new cattle dairy farms that have been developed by the DDA in Madanpur Khadar, Masoodpur, and Khichripur. About 12,000 cattle have been relocated.

The old markets, like those of Motia Khan and subzimandi, have now passed into history. In their places have arisen new vistas, new markets, like those of Naraina and Azadpur, bouncing with new energy and looking to future with confidence. In many other spheres, old has given place to new. The Seventh Delhi has been relieved of some of the albatrosses around its neck, while Eighth Delhi has been saved from being overcrowded. This is by no means a small contribution of Ninth Delhi.

In any economy, there is a competing demand on resources. This is particularly so in a developing country like India. Here, major portions of the resources are needed for investment in agriculture, industry, power and the like; and it is not possible to make available any significant portion of the resources for direct investment in development and improvement of city.

To meet the challenge of resources, Ninth Delhi evolved innovative, almost revolutionary, techniques of financing city development programme. The three major components of these techniques are: setting up of a revolving fund of Rs 5 crores; ensuring that full benefits of the infrastructural investment made by the public authorities are reaped by them; and mopping up of marginal saving in the community by stimulating man's instinct of saving for the house.

The operation of revolving fund to secure large-scale acquisition of land with a small initial capital has already been indicated. The development projects undertaken by the DDA can be divided into the following three broad categories:

Category I—Projects which are remunerative, such as construction of shopping and office complexes and development of residential plots for comparatively higher income groups.

Category II—Projects which are not remunerative but from which full cost can be recovered, such as provision of plots and houses for the middle-income group.

Category III—Unremunerative projects, such as subsidized housing for the poorer section and development of "green" areas, setting up of new woodlands and parks and landscaping of sites around monuments of historical and cultural importance.

The mechanism of revolving fund was so used that surpluses accruing from projects of Category I were balanced against the deficiencies of projects of Category III, and a self-generating process of integrated and balanced development was set in motion.

Setting up of revolving fund would not by itself have provided the additional resources. Simultaneously, it was ensured that the economic advantage, accruing from the infrastructure created by investment of a part of the revolving fund, was fully reaped by the DDA and utilized for financing further projects of acquisition and development. If, for instance, investment made by the DDA from the revolving fund in constructing roads and opening new areas had not been accompanied by advance "freezing" or acquisition of land, advantage of that investment would have been taken by the speculators. In almost all other metropolitan centres of developing countries, including India, it has often happened that investment made from national resources for creation of infrastructures in the cities has been exploited by a few vested interests.

Even a poor man has scope for saving. Undoubtedly, he will have to make some sacrifice to effect saying. And he may be willing to do that, provided he gets some benefit in return, say a house on hire-purchase basis, after a couple of years. Recognition of this simple fact by the DDA has enabled it to raise Rs 10 crores for its public housing programme by securing from the intending buyers advance deposits equivalent to a small percentage of the cost.

From these innovative techniques, the details of which cannot obviously be discussed here, a number of advantages accrued. First, growth of a planned and balanced city which reflects the total personality of man and answers all his needs— economic, social, cultural and recreational—is facilitated. Secondly, developed urban lands become available, which can be distributed in accordance with the needs of the different sections of the community. Thirdly, by holding promises of allotment of a house, even marginal savings are mopped up, and seed-capital secured for initiating public housing programme. Fourthly, allotment on hire-purchase basis instils a habit of forced saving and sets in deflationary tendencies in the economy.

TRAGEDIES

All these developments represent the triumphs of Ninth Delhi. But it has its tragedies too. In our cities, civic consciousness and pride are conspicuous by their absence. Nor is there firm national commitment to solve their ever increasing problems.

Let me illustrate the position by referring to the cases of a Chinese city and an Indian city. This was the picture of Shanghai in "pre-revolutionary China" 27 years ago:

In addition to the familiar evils of slums and inhuman overcrowding, of mass unemployment, of filth, disorder and mass mendicancy, there was a particular shamelessness of fights and crimes and exploitation in the old Shanghai.[3]

And this is what is Shanghai now:

The city is still over-crowded, but not intolerably so; it is a city of cleanliness, order and cooperation. It is a working city again, not an out-of-control agglomeration of mankind. An "exploding city" has been defused and contained, and is now being reformed and regenerated.[4]

On the other hand, this is how Calcutta scene was described by Rudyard Kipling about 80 years ago:

As the fungus sprouts chaotic from its bed,
So it spread....
And above the packed and pestilential town
Death looked down.

The current scene is not very different:

Calcutta and its attendant towns and districts now stretch like a rotting narrow ribbon for sixty miles along the foetid banks of the Hoogly river, and in every possible way that a city can go sour, this has gone sourer... and estimated 600,000 sleep in the streets every night. Almost half of the suffocatingly populous area is totally without sewers, and even a moderate shower floods the shallow kutcha channels which act as drains, and sweeps the filth and effluent through thousands of bustee basements, and even middle-class kitchens.[5]

In China, there has been firm national policy and commitment, and results have been encouraging. In India, on the other hand, we are still in a state of draft. We know that we are faced with a problem of unprecedented magnitude. Our metropolitan cities are getting urbanized rapidly without acquiring even an iota of the capacity to absorb the in-coming population. Yet we do nothing to evolve and implement an effective policy of balanced regional growth. It is not necessary that we follow the Chinese model. France and Rumania have successfully implemented policies of regional development by following methods other than those of China. What we need is a national commitment, a motivation to improve and develop. One of the tragedies of Ninth Delhi has been its inability to generate civic consciousness and pride and involve the neighbouring state governments in overall national commitment to plan and develop the city as a part of the metropolitan region.

We also know that urban as well as urbanizable land is a valuable asset. Its imaginative use can provide the much-needed resources for solving the problems of our cities. But what do we do? We allow our assets to be converted into liabilities. Instead of using lands in a planned way to secure the maximum advantage, stinking, haphazard slums are allowed to crop up, which endanger the health of the community, lower its overall productivity, and burden the posterity with huge financial liability. Should there not be a firm national commitment to ensure that resources are not wasted in this manner?

Another tragedy of almost catastrophic dimensions has been the emergence of a new class of saboteurs. Ninth Delhi has been betrayed by this class. The new class did not comprise capitalists or rich colonizers, but new racketeers, mostly drawn from the crafty, greedy and power hungry nucleus of the middle class which was quick to perceive and exploit the inherent weaknesses of our social and political set-up. It evolved a new technique of speculating on urban lands, and acquiring, in the process, both financial and political power. A posture of helping the poor, and serving the cause of humanism, was assumed. Within the "poor" a class was created, whose interests were aligned with those of the new class. The subsidiary partner was attracted by the prospects of securing lands at "stolen property rates" and investing their unaccounted money in free-hold lands from which still larger profits could be reaped subsequently.

The *modus operandi* was subtle. Lands in the urban areas or on their fringes were cornered through "agreement" to purchase or other crafty devices. It was immaterial whether the land was notified for acquisition or earmarked for a different use in the master plan. Those who did not part with the lands were either made partners, though with a smaller percentage of the booty, or coerced into submission through agents. Soon thereafter, all such lands were divided into small plots and sold at very high price on the "map" by equally crafty means of booking of execution of "power of attorney." No development was carried out. Practically, no land was left for any community facility. Invariably, deception was carefully planned. Through hired agents, potential value of the land was propagated. To raise land values, some electric poles were got dug or bricks placed along kutcha path. The buyers, too, came from these segment of the community who had black or unaccounted money and posed as poor people.

The new class grew imperceptibly out of the new power structure which started operating at the local level. It first secured political foothold by jumping on somebody's bandwagons. Then it extended its power by acquiring finances through illegal sale of lands and by encouraging unauthorized construction. It consolidated its position by establishing contacts at lower and middle level of administration and acquiring, in the process, powers to blackmail and intimidate officers at higher level. It sold not only lands but also techniques of avoiding action by obtaining stay orders and delaying the cases till the structures could be proclaimed old and their demolition assailed on humanitarian grounds.

To begin with, the new class had a few recruits. But as the advantages, political and personal, became obvious, its rank swelled, and it became a powerful force. The "marauders" framed a subtle strategy, keeping in view the indifference, superficiality and lack of civic consciousness of the people.

The new class is a real tyrant, all the more oppressive and dangerous because it operates behind the scene. It is a class which has done incalculable damage not only to the landscape of the city but also to its spiritual fabric. It has spread baser values and caused widespread misuse of institutions. It combines the worst traits of a speculator and a blackmailer. Some of its members have acquired vast wealth and political power to manipulate. In the case of Najafgarh Road, not less than Rs 80 lakhs is believed to have been pocketed by a member of this class by employing techniques stated above.

This, in brief, is the story of Ninth Delhi, its legacy, its triumphs and tragedies.

Island and its Future

In this and preceding chapters, I have endeavoured to provide you with some glimpses of my island of truth, an island which must be viewed in the context of its totality, its climate, its values, its desire to break shackles of routine and technicality and eliminate hidden inhumanity and injustice. You may have had a look at its landmarks, its green vistas, and its hundreds of new colonies and estates. You may have also felt the sulking presence of a new class of racketeers, keenly waiting for an opportunity to surprise and throttle the sentinels and ravish the youthful buoyancy of the island.

Your sojourn with me on my island may have acquainted you with a tormented soul battered by calumny and injustice. Some people have often asked me as to why I take criticism of the DDA as my personal criticism. I have seldom tried to answer this question. Those who do not know what commitment is, what involvement is, are not likely to understand. The truth is that I have never been disturbed by any bonafide criticism. What has anguished me is the malicious, almost sadistic, pleasure which some people derive in running down the DDA, primarily because it did not play to the tune of vested interests, and was keen to look beneath the surface and also to the times ahead. To me, the DDA has always been, and still is, like a child. If you mock his tattered clothes, because he cannot afford better ones, I am pained. If, like street urchins, you throw stones at him, because he does not join them, I feel hurt. If you break the roadside lamp under which he is working to equip himself better to fight the battle of poverty and underdevelopment, I shed silent tears. It is not criticism, not even lack of sympathy and understanding, but the propensity to hurt, to denigrate, to frustrate, to mislead, that pains.

Whatever it may be—sentimentality, commitment or involvement—it is there. It is the truth. I have never tried to hide it. Unfortunately, most people have the habit of measuring others by their own values. Whatever you may think, I have genuinely been attracted by the following words which Lutyen proposed for inscription on Jaipur columns in New Delhi:

Endow your thoughts with Faith

Ninth Delhi

> Your deeds with courage
> Your life with sacrifice
> So all men may know
> The greatness of India

Whether one succeeds or fails, is a different matter. In some cases, "fate fulfils what faith wills"; in other cases, it does not. In any case, the tragedy of a single individual or single institution is not of much consequence. The issues involved are far more basic. The future of the city, future of the nation, depends upon them. Are we going to face the reality or play with its images? When we are in swamp, does it make any sense that we should engage ourselves in throwing mud at one another? Is it not prudent that we first come out of the swamp, secure a foothold on the dry land and use it as a launching pad to usher in an era of real justice and real truth? Are we going to protect our shallowness like a treasure and not change our administrative ethos and institutions which frustrate rather than secure justice to the people and the community? How is it that before the emergency, thousands were engaged in illegal constructions with the connivance of a new class, and how is it they suddenly disappeared from the scene during the emergency? Why is it that the ravagers have now reappeared inflicting thousands of wounds on the landscape of the city and tearing to pieces whatever remained of the moral fabric of the community? In this context, is issue or non-issue of notices the only planning value which we are going to cherish?

These are disturbing questions but must be faced, if we have to come anywhere near the ideals of a fair and just city, a fair and just state. At present, we seem to have lost our moorings. Uncertainty haunts us like an approaching storm. I am not sure about the future of my island. Is it going to be eroded and wiped out of existence or is it going to serve as a lighthouse to tottering ships on a rough sea?

EPILOGUE

Delhi—My Delhi*
(Songs of Truth)

In your green lawns of my vision
I walked erect
The buoyant air lifted my curly head
Young flowers smiled with sweet majesty
And I laughed
But time has blurred the vision of my youth
And faded the freshness of my mind
Pale leaves fall off one by one
Rub against the chillness of my feet
And murmur the loss of innocent hope.

Your crowded halls
Your busy streets
I leave alone
And move
Along the shadows of your dreadful walls
Into the darkness of your slums
The slums of human shape
The slums of human faith
There I cross my weary legs and stop
Set the broken hair on my ageing head
Lean on the mirror of my cruel thoughts
And talk forbidden things to myself.

Your real soul is in stinking drains
Your real mind is in dirty lanes
The ancient rubbish lies all around

*Courtesy: *Illustrated Weekly of India* in which this poem (larger version) first appeared.

Epilogue

Its wanton breeze
Feeds the empty brains of oldish rogues
Saps God's freshness in Mother's womb
Corrupts the incorruptible
From the corners of your smoky dens
The dirty rags of your existence
Are thrown naked one by one
Rolling their yellow faces
In the dusty bosom of your burning sun
In these soulless domes of humanity
In these cemeteries of our living men
Ghosts of future progress walk
While we indulge in our fashionable talk
Of doing this and that.

On the other side in your lighted kingdom
Your youthful pride
Your new-born babe
Caesared out of the aged womb
Of ignorance and shame
Heaves the scented air of freedom
Leaps around with vacant mind
And grows—
His eyes are stony
And do not blink
At the sullen faces that lean
And the empty hands
That raise the dirty plates
In luxurious grooves
Of air-conditioned rooms
The doors of which sometimes creak
And bring in hawking boys' shriek
To disturb only the rustling music
Of spoons and plates
And perhaps the little smoke
That curls around some listless pipes
Lifts its ears and then dies.

Why then look around and pride
In foreign mansions of foreign times?

Why tread on soft shining grass
Or boom our cars on fleshy paths
And breathe the air of progress?
Why jump in crowded streets
And clap with joy
The few mighty minds of our times?
Why ignore the voice of History
And live in the world of make-belief?

Why not sing the songs of truth
And say
In your slums of human faiths
Mighty minds come and go
But your dirty lanes remain
And your stinking drains flow.

JAGMOHAN

NOTES

CHAPTER I

[1] My office was located at a distance of three miles from Jhandewalan.
[2] Town and Country Planning Organization (TCPO) Report (Jhuggi-Jhonpri), 1973.

CHAPTER II

[1] Barbara Ward, *Home of Man*, United Nations, Habitat, May 1976, Vancouvre, Canada.
[2] United Nations, *World Housing Survey*, 1974, p. 28.
[3] T. Vittachi, quoted from *Mankind at the Turning Point* by Micajilo Mesarovic and Edward Pastel, p. 80.
[4] See author's "A New Human Settlement," *Hindustan Times*, April 1972.
[5] TCPO Report (Jhuggi-Jhonpri), 1973.

CHAPTER III

[1] *Indian Express*, 20 June 1967.
[2] *Statesman*, 20 June 1967.
[3] *Illustrated Weekly of India*, 7 March 1971.
[4] Public Accounts Committee Report, 1971-72.
[5] *Statesman*, 1 July 1967.

CHAPTER V

[1] Labour cost constitutes 40 per cent of the total cost of the house.
[2] D.V. Rao, "Public Sector Investment as a Tool for Larger Private Sector Participation," *Journal of Town Planners*, June 1973, p. 2.
[3] TCPO Report (Jhuggi-Jhonpri), 1973.

CHAPTER VIII

[1] Report (1974), Town Planner, DDA.
[2] Marshall B. Clinard, *Slums and Community Development*, p. 74.
[3] Jagmohan, *Rebuilding Shahjahanabad: The Walled City of Delhi*, pp. 32-33.
[4] Taking the estimate cost of tenements as Rs 15,000 (including land).
[5] 81,300 families in Ward I to II; 80,000 families in Ward XII to XIV; 35,000 families in Ward XV; 23,000 families in Ward XVI; 12,000 families in Ward XVIII and other areas. These figures are based on 1971 census and do not include future population.
[6] This meeting was also attended by R.C. Jain, the then Special Assistant to the Lieutenant Governor.

CHAPTER IX

[1] F. Bernian, *Travels in Mughal Empire 1656-1668*, p. 246.
[2] A.P. Hume, *Report on Relief of Congestion in Delhi*.
[3] Quoted from the Conference Report on the Exploding Cities, Oxford, 2-6 April 1974. See Neville Maxwell's Chapter "The City in China" in the report.
[4] *Ibid.*
[5] Peter Wilshen and Roseman Righton, "The Noise and the Smell of the People," *Exploding Cities*, p. 8.

APPENDIXES

APPENDIXES

APPENDIX I

DEMOLITION FROM 26 SEPTEMBER 1977 TO 31 MARCH 1978 (POST-EMERGENCY)

Date of demolition	Locality	Number of structures demolished
26. 9.1977	Motia Khan	75
27. 9.1977	Geeta Colony	150
6.10.1977	Majnu-ka-Tila	96
7.10.1977	Pusa Road and Kitchner Road	16
10.10.1977	Bela Estate	150
14.10.1977	Bela Estate	270
17.10.1977	Lawrence Road and Gujrawala township	50
18.10.1977	New Subzimandi, Azadpur and Azadpur Bus Terminal	2315
31.10.1977	East of Kailash	10
3.11.1977	Azadpur Subzimandi	100
19.11.1977	Yakutpur	8
24.11.1977	Lawrence Road and New Subzimandi	173
2.12.1977	Azadpur Subzimandi	200
3.12.1977	Wazirpur	60
4.12.1977 to 6.12.1977	Azadpur Subzimandi	clearance
8.12.1977	Madangir	182
9.12.1977	Azadpur Subzimandi Mori Gate	61
13.12.1977	R.K. Puram	126
14.12.1977	Rajinder Nagar, Shanker Road, Dus Gaon, Todapur	38
16.12.1977	Pandoo Nagar	60
17.12.1977	Tughlakabad	5
27.12.1977	Aliganj Khureji Khas	20
11. 1.1978	Mandawla Road	2
17. 1.1978	Jhandewalan M M Road and Motia Khan	102
18. 1.1978	Ashok Vihar, Phases I and III	105
19. 1.1978	R.K. Puram	65
20. 1.1978	Jhandewalan	94
28. 1.1978	I.S.B.T. Complex	15
1. 2.1978	Madangir	50
2. 2.1978	Janakpuri	34

3. 2.1978	Janakpuri	60
15. 2.1978	Trilokpuri	91
17. 2.1978	Nangal Rai, Aliganj, Jangpura	115
22. 2.1978	Majhadpur and Himayunpur Kalu Sarai	82
23. 2.1978	Kalkaji Housing Complex	38
25. 2.1978	K.W. Camp	35
28. 2.1978	Bela Estate	165
1. 3.1978	Jamuna Bazar, Punjabi Bagh, Shakurpur, Rishi Nagar, Shanti Nagar	153
6. 3.1978	Singlipur, Sahaipur Shalimar Bagh Scheme	50
9. 3.1978	Lawrence Road	24
10. 3.1978	Sarai Pipalthala	11
13. 3.1978	Subzimandi Azadpur	500
14. 3.1978	Chiragh Janubi	11
20. 3.1978	Friends Colony	17
22. 3.1978	Ashok Vihar	15
27. 3.1978	New Subzimandi	200
28. 3.1978	Raghubir Nagar	1
31. 3.1978	New Subzimandi	56
	TOTAL	6263

Whereas during the emergency, no arrests were made, no tear gas was bursted, except in Turkman Gate area where, as shown in Chapter VIII, riots occurred due to reasons other than "clearance." In the post-emergency period, a large number of arrests have been made and tear gas and lathi-charges resorted to on a number of occasions. For instance, in respect of DDA demolition operations alone about one hundred arrests were made.

APPENDIX II

Name of the witness	Property number	Reference of acquisition, etc.	Number of alternative plots/flats obtained against each property
Zahirud-din	3339	Annexure C Serial No. 8 of the list (Award No. 1044/1258 dt. 30.6.53)	8
Ramjani	3277	Annexure C Sl. No. 15: Award money paid vide resolution No. 335 dt., 23.8.1938	12
Jamila Begum	3319	List of acquired property (page 9)	9
Ibrahim	3301-4	Shifted at his request given in writing. Got a middle income group flat from the DDA	10
Islam-ud-din	Q. No. 13 (Transit Camp)	DDA's property: The entire Transit Camp was constructed by the DDA	2
Smt. Anaro	3387	Sr. No. 18 Annexure D Award money paid vide resolution No. 335 dated 23.8.1938	12
Jamal-ud-din	3358	Sr. No. 13 Annexure C Award No. 875/1260 dt. 27.12.1949	15
Bashir-udin Shafi	3305	Annexure A Sr. No. 29, Award No. 1003/1237, dt. 27.4.51	15

Jahadin	3299	Person claiming himself as manager (not owner) appeared. In respect of this property, a registered notice was sent by the DDA, during the emergency, asking the party to submit documents within a prescribed period failing which the case would be closed. No document was furnished and case was filed	22
		TOTAL	105

APPENDIX III

EXTRACTS FROM MY WRITTEN STATEMENT
IN RESPECT OF:

(i) *Sultanpuri Majra*

On 29 May 1976, the DDA field staff contacted the occupants of the unauthorized structures and explained to them that, since their structures were unauthorized and liable to be demolished, it would be in their interest to secure allotment in the resettlement colony of Sultanpuri. It was also explained to them that those who moved early would be able to secure allotment at advantageous location.

After the distribution of demolition/allotment slips, the allottees moved to the allotted sites voluntarily and according to their own convenience. No demolition squad went to the site. The process of shifting extended over a period exceeding seven to eight months. No force or coercion was exercised by the DDA staff. This is borne out of the fact that, even though allotment slips were distributed in May 1976, a large number of structures are still standing at the site. If force or coercion had been exercised, such structures could not have continued to exist.

(ii) *Jahangirpuri/Peepal Thala*

At the time of survey on 16 May 1976, the DDA field staff contacted the residents of the occupied houses and explained to them that, since the structures were unauthorized and liable to be demolished, it would be in their interest to secure allotment either in the resettlement colony of Jahangirpuri or in any other residential colony or housing estate of the DDA. It was also explained to them that those who moved early would be able to secure allotment at advantageous locations. Those who had larger area were given two or more allotment slips. Some of them were given plots of 40 to 80 sq. yds. or LIG/MIG flats.

After the distribution of demolition/allotment slips, the allottees moved to the allotted sites according to their own convenience. No demolition squad went to the site. The movement of the allottees was voluntary. No force or coercion was exercised by the DDA staff. This is borne out by the fact that, even though allotment slips were distributed in May 1976, more than 200 structures are still standing at the site. Some of the structures are right in the middle of the road and obstructing the process of development. Even then, these structures were not removed. If force or coercion had been exercised, such structures could not have continued to exist.

There has been no forcible occupation of land. The lands of Peepal Thala had been acquired long ago. Only the award had to be up-dated by adding interest till date. Since this was advantageous to the villagers, they did not object. The compensation was paid after adding the requisite interest.

(*iii*) "*Temple*" (*Green Park*)

In this case, an unauthorized structure was demolished, alongwith other (70) unauthorized structures in the Arjan Nagar area in September 1975. It is also clear that

(*a*) What to speak of getting building plans sanctioned, no one even cared to submit any plan at all;

(*b*) The unauthorized structure was put up in the alignment of an important road;

(*c*) There is no registered sale or gift deed in favour of the person or party who have complained to the Commission;

(*d*) No one gave any intimation about such a building having been constructed; and

(*e*) The clearance operation in Arjan Nagar area began on 23 September 1975 and structure in question was cleared on 25 September 1975. What prevented the person interested in the building in approaching me or any other senior officers of the DDA with the intimation that a "temple" had been put up and the same might not be cleared?

When the deputation of Sarvadeshik Arya Pratinidhi Sabha met me, I told them that the allotment for a regular temple at concessional rate could be made, provided certain terms and conditions were fulfilled. The Sabha agreed to comply with the conditions and allotment of 1,200 sq. yds. of land was made to them.

In respect of the Lt. Governor's instructions about the demolition of "religious" buildings, it is clear that these instructions apply only to the genuine, old, and established religious buildings. The matter had, in fact, been clarified as far back as December 1972.

(*iv*) *Kapas Hera*

In respect of the demolition/clearance in Kapas Hera area on 4, 17 and 18 September 1975, the DDA's role was limited to

(*a*) making available the services of the central demolition squad as per instructions (1967) of the Delhi Administration/Central Government and in accordance with the normal practice in vogue before the emergency; and

(*b*) Offering alternative accommodation to help the persons affected, though they were unauthorized builders and not legally entitled to such accommodation, in resettling themselves at appropriate places.

I also refer to the minutes of the meeting held under the Chairmanship of the then Lt. Governor Baleshwar Prasad, on 18 April 1972. In this meeting, it was, inter alia, reiterated by the Lt. Governor that "the demolition squad of the DDA could be pressed in service whenever needed by any agency and there was no use wasting resources on duplicating such arrangements."

The DDA has been making available (before the emergency) the services of the demolition squad to various agencies. In support of this assertion, four specific instances are cited.

I have acted in accordance with the government's policy and instructions and in accordance with the practice in vogue before the emergency. Even now, i.e. after the emergency, the same policy, instructions and pratices are being followed. Unfortunately, even educated and well-placed persons like the proprietors of Nu Foam Industry and Paper Products have, for pecuniary and personal benefits, got into the habit of not even caring to submit building plans to the competent local authorities, what to speak of securing proper sanction of the building plans, etc.

I have, in fact, helped the persons affected to obtain alternative plots in conforming and approved colonies, and thus set them on the path of progress and prosperity. Establishment of industries in conforming areas is not only in public interest but also help the industrialists to expand their projects and acquire higher productivity.

(v) *Arjan Nagar Area*

The unauthorized structures cleared in the area in question fall in the following two categories:

(a) Land (about 14 acres)/structures in respect of which action was taken by the Land Acquisition Collector who acquired the land, in pursuance of the scheme sanctioned by the Central Government, and took over the possession in accordance with the normal practice in vogue and provision of the Land Acquisition Act;

(b) Structures, spread over about two acres of land, in respect of which action to demolish unauthorized construction was taken under the Delhi Development Act. The constructions had been put up without getting the building plans sanctioned as was statutorily required. (The unauthorized builders did not even care to submit building plans.) The possession of the land falling in this category was not taken.

As illustration of the procedure and practice, I may invite the attention of the Commission to the two cases in which possession of land in village Badarpur and that of land in village Gonda Neemka Banger was taken over, before the emergency, on 7 December 1974 and 2 February 1974 respectively in the same manner as has been done in the case of Arjan Nagar.

No deviation from the usual procedure, in vogue before the emergency, has taken place. What the DDA has really done is to help people affected by the operation in resettling themselves at appropriate places. The concessions of resettlement were in addition to the compensation payable to the claimants as per awards of the Court. Thus, the persons affected have been more liberally treated than the legal provision justify.

In regard to the allotment of flats to the occupants of unauthorized structures demolished in Arjan Nagar, I submit that it is incorrect that no such allotment was made prior to the case of Arjan Nagar or prior to emergency. The following two precedents are cited:

(a) A number of occupants of land near Picnic Hut, Hauz Khas, were allotted flats in village Katwaria Sarai. A copy of the relevant note including the note, dated 18 February 1974 of the then Lt. Governor, Baleshwar Prasad, is enclosed.

(b) The evictees of Kashmir House were also allotted flats in 1974.

In respect of the alleged allotments of flats to Arjan Dass's "relations," I submit that I had given only general approval of the list of the persons who, according to the recommendations, were eligible for allotment in terms of the policy decision taken with the approval of the Lieutenant Governor and the Housing Committee. Apart from the fact that the individual cases were not to be decided by me, unless someone made a representation, the list could not reveal the alleged relationship. Further, when the recommendations were put up to me, they were accompanied by an additional safeguard. i.e. filing of the prescribed affidavit. If anyone gave false affidavit, it was he who ran the risk of prosecution. All cases were covered by a uniform policy decision and over dozen flats were also allotted in many other cases to independent families living in a single house.

INDEX

Abbas, Khwaja Ahmed, 90
Ad hoc Slum Clearance Committee (1964), 34, 35, 136
Aggarwal, D.K., member of the Fact Finding Committee, 96; role in clearance operation, 103
Ahmed, Fakhruddin Ali, 88, 89
Ahmed, Mir Mushtaq, and Yamuna Bazar Clearance Operation, 35; statement on Turkman Gate incident, 147, 148
Alam, Khurshid, letter to Vice-Chairman, DDA, relating to slum-dwellers around Jamia Millia, 51
An Eye to India by David Selbourne, concocted story in, 82
Anand, Mulk Raj, complaints against slum-dwellers around Hauz Khas, 52
Asia, problem of squatters in, 20

Bajwa, K.S., deposition before the Shah Commission, 149
Bakht, Sikander, 96, 100
Banerji, A.N., 45, 84
Bansal, S.N., on unauthorized encroachments, 110, 111
Bernier, 177
Bhagat, H.K.L., 48, 89-90; on resettlement colonies, 50
Blitz, report on Trilokpuri complex, 93
Bombay, squatter problem in, 20
Brahm Prakash, member of the Squatter Resettlement Scheme, 28

Brodie, J.A., 173
Bukhari, Syed Abdullah, Friday speech on sterilization issue, 145, 148
Bulldozers, use before and during emergency, 70-72, 127, 150, 155, 156; practice of deployment, 156
Bureaucracy, ethos of, 95, 113, 114; Shah Commission's attitude towards, 4-6

Calcutta, case study of, 183, 184; pavement conditions in, 22; squatter problem in, 20
Cattle milk dairy farms, development of, 15, 180, 181; Task Force recomendation for, 51
Clearance-cum-resettlement operation, procedures of, 17; *see also* Resettlement colonies
Charles, Prince, on the development of the River Front, 16
Chavan, Y.B., 35
Chawla, Navin, deposition before Shah Commission, 84, 85
Chawri Bazar Scheme, Tamta's role in, 88
Chiragh Delhi, clearance of, 43
Choudhury, Des Raj, member of the Squatter Resettlement Scheme, 28
City, classification of, 170, 171; perspective of, 171-75
City forests, creation of, 11; *see also* Ninth Delhi and Resettlement colonies

Commercial squatters, role of, 38, 39; *see also* Squatters
Commission of Inquiry Act, 109
Commission of Inquiry Rules, 107
Curzon, Lord, on Indian bureaucracy, 113

Decline and Fall of Indira Gandhi by Mankekar, concocted story in, 3, 79, 80
Defence of India Rule, demand for the use of, 41
Delhi, campaign to bring about planned and balanced development of, 10; environment of historical places, 10; existing problems of, 15; historical perspective of, 171, 172; observations on the development of, 15, 16; squatter household, yearwise statistics, 24; woodlands, creation of, 11; *see also* Ninth Delhi
Delhi Development Act, 1957, 27, 166, 167
DDA officers, predicament of, 116-18; R.C. Jain's attempt to obtain incriminating statements from, 99-102
Delhi Under Emergency by Dayal and Bose, concocted story in, 80, 81
Demolitions of structures in 1977, 8
Developing countries, problems of squatters in, 19, 20
Devgun, Hardayal, on Yamuna Bazar Clearance Operation, 35
Dhar, P.N., 46
Dharama Vira, 32, 105, 174
Dhaula Kuan site, Tourism Ministry's request for clearance of, 51
Dixit, S.C., 102
Dixit, Uma Shankar, 40

Experiment with Untruth by Michael Henderson, concocted story in, 81, 82

Fact Finding Committee, 96, 99, 106, 117; appointment of, 96; criticism of, 109, 110, 117; members of, 96; Jagmohan's views on, 100
Family Planning campaign, 143, 144, 151, 169; and riots, 126, 127; Magistrate's report on, 149
Fruit and vegetable market, Azadpur, construction of, 11, 15

Galbraith, Professor, 14; on historical perspective of city, 171
Gandhi, Indira, 168; on unauthorized encroachments, 41, 54, 55; statement in the Rajya Sabha, 48; surprise visit to resettlement colonies, 49
Gandhi, Mahatma, 169; on the condition of Indian villages, 23
Gandhi, Sanjay, 3, 78, 118, 169; interview to an American journalist, 3
Ghata Masjid, clearance of, 37
Ghazipur cattle resettlement colony, 75
Gujaral, I.K., 42, 50
Gurwari Moti Bagh, clearance of, 37
Gupta, Hans Raj, 33; member of the Squatter Resettlement Scheme, 28
Gupta, Kanwarlal, member of the Squatter Resettlement Scheme, 28; on Yamuna Bazar Clearance Operation, 35
Gupta, Shiv Charan, arrest during the Yamuna Bazar operation, 34; member of the Squatter Resettlement Scheme, 28

Haksar, P.N., 50
Hanuman Temple, clearance operation in, 36

Index

Haussmann, Baron, 174
Housing problem, magnitude of, 22

Idgah clearance operation, 36, 37
Illegal sales, of land, increase of, 40; action against, 40, 41
India, squatter population rate in, 20
INA area clearance, 43
Indian cities, standard of open spaces, compared with American and English lawns, 15
Indian villages, poor conditions of, 22, 23
Industrial estates, development of, 10, 11
Inter-State Bus Terminus, construction of, 11

Jagmohan, attempt to defame, 96, 99, 101, 114-16; case registered against, 100, 101; CBI inquiry against, 96; Cultural Award to, 45; from a national hero to a national villain, 104, 105; R.C, Jain's hostile attitude towards, 17, 96-104; Padma Shri, Padma Bhushan awarded to, 105; propaganda against, 96, 114-16; subtle hints to become an "approver," 105; suspension orders, 104
Jain, R.C., apppointed as Special Assistant to Lieutenant-Governor, 42, 43, 97; hostile attitude towards Jagmohan, 17, 96-104; member of the Fact Finding Committee, 96; role in VIP Land Grab Scandal, 97-99; weakness for residential plots, 97
Jama Masjid Complex, redevelopment of, 49-52
Jha, Dr A.N., 35, 44, 105, 175; member of the Squatter Resettlement Scheme, 28; role in Yamuna Bazar Clearance Operation, 32
Jhandewalan, clearance of, 11, 43, 51

Judgement by Kuldip Nayar, false story about Turkman Gate in, 77, 122

Kabari market, shifting of, 15
Kayam-u-din, 3; evidence before Shah Commission on Turkman Gate incident, 6
Kela Godown, clearance of, 37
Khandawala, Kari, 117
Khanna, Mehar Chand, 34, 35
Khichripur-Trilokpuri-Kalyanpuri Complex, 64-69
Khosla, Dr J.N., 105
Kishan Chand, 73, 151; deposition before Shah Commission, 83-86; Old Subzi Mandi clearance operation under his supervision, 45, 46
Kotla Ferozeshah, clearance of, 37
Kripalani, J.B., complaint against slum-dwellers, 52

Lal, H.K., 88, 157
Lal, Kishore, demand for the use of DIR, 41, 42; on Yamuna Bazar Clearance Operation, 34
Le Corbusier, role in building Chandigarh, 174
Lekhi, P.N., government counsel to the Commission, 6, 117
Low and middle-income group houses, 10, 11
Lutyen, Edwin, 172-74

Mainstream, Inder Mohan's concocted article in, 79.
Maintenance of Internal Security Act, 5; demand for the use of, 41
Malhotra, Vijay Kumar, 96; and Yamuna Bazar Clearance Operation, 33; member of the Squatter Resettlement Scheme, 28; on the emergence of unauthorized colonies, 42
Mangolpuri resettlement colony, 30
Master Plan (1962-1981), 27, 28

Mayo, Katherine, 82, 172
Mehta, Om, 46
Migration, process of, 24, 25
Mirdha, Ram Niwas, 46
Mishra, Bibhuti, on Yamuna Bazar Clearance Operation, 35
Mohan, Inder, and Turkman Gate incident, 122; concocted story of, 77, 78; deposition before Shah Commission, 5
Mohsin, 151; deposition before Shah Commission, 88, 89
Motia Khan Market, shifting of, 49, 151
Mountbatten, Lord, on the beautification of Delhi, 16
Mukerjee, Debabratta, VIP Land Grab Scandal Case and verdict of, 98, 99
Mukerjee, Nirmal, 45

Naqvi, S.H., 148
Nehru, Jawaharlal, 128; idea of setting up of a single planned development authority, 26; interest in the planned development of the city, 174; on Delhi city, 172; support in the construction of Chandigarh, 174
Nehru Place, commercial and business centre, 11
New Delhi, story of the construction of, 173, 174
Nigam Bodh Ghat, change in the environment of, 33
Ninth Delhi, development efforts, 175, 176; development projects, 181; element of social justice, 176; emergence of new centres of commercial and institutional activity, 180, 181; features of, 176; housing schemes of, 178; "mini forests" and woodlands in, 179; operation of revolving fund, 181, 182; planning foundation of, 175; planning values and natural landscape, 179; problems of, 174, 175; tragedies of, 184-86; triumphs of, 175-82; statistics relating to residential plots and houses, 178

Ohri, R.K., deposition before Shah Commission, 149
Old Subzi Mandi Clearance Operation, 45, 46
Over-population, impact of, 14
Over-urbanization, impact of, 14

Pandav Nagar, clearance of, 43
Parliamentary Consultative Committee, 4; programme of clearance and resettlement and, 49, 50
Piracha, Siraj, 79; evidence before Shah Commission on Turkman Gate, 5
Plantation of trees, 11; *see also* Resettlement colonies
Politics, 17; and slums, 34-36
Pradhan, Ashok, evidence before Shah Commission, 148
Prasad, Dr Rajendra, letter to Chief Commissioner relating to Nigam Bodh Ghat, 31, 32
Prasad Nagar clearance operation (1968), 37
Propaganda, 95, 96, 114-16
Public Accounts Committee, 124; praise for resettling squatters, 37
Public Premises Act, 69, 133

Racketeers, 95; efforts to curb, 47; emergence of, 184; *modus operandi* of, 185, 186
Raghuramiah, K., evidence before Shah Commission, 4
Rajindra Place, compared to Connaught Place, 11
Rama Krishna Purama, clearance of, 67
Raman, Radha, on the achievement of DDA, 48, 49
Rampur, clearance of, 43
Report of the Slum Department of DDA (1975), 137

Index

Resettlement Colonies, bank loan facilities to, 13, 14, 62-64; community halls, construction of, 13; culverts, development and statistics of, 13; DDA's socialist measures, 17, 18, 50-54; dispensaries, construction of, 13; drains, development of, 13; employment opportunities, provision of, 13, 62-64; funds required for, 164; hand-pumps, development and statistics of, 13; higher secondary school building, construction of, 13; lavatory seats construction of, 13; milk bars, facilities of, 13; new pattern and features of, 15, 72-76; parks, development of, 13; plantation, 11, 13; progress during the emergency, 49-51; residential plots, 12, 13; shop-plots, development of, 13; super bazars, construction of, 13; TV sheds, construction of, 13; tube-wells, development and statistics of, 13; violation of Master Plan in, 92, 93; water supply lines, development of, 13

Resettlement sites, criteria adopted in selection of, 64

Residential plots, development of, 10, 11

Resources, paucity of, 14, 23

Sahni, Kidar Nath, member of the Squatter Resettlement Scheme, 28; on unauthorized colonies, 42; on the false story about Malhotra-Jagmohan relationship, 96

Saini, Miss Surinder, member of the Squatter Resettlement Scheme, 28

Sait, Ibrahim Sulaiman, 145, 146

Sarai Rohilla Bridge, clearance of, 51, 59

Shah Commission, 47, 115, 116; denial of the right to cross-examination at the "assistance stage," 106, 107; misgivings about procedures of, 108, 109; terms of reference of, 107, 108

Shahjahanabad, conditions of, 177; problems of, 167, 168

Sahay, Bhagwan, 32, 92, 105, 174

Saxena, deposition before Shah Commission, 149

Seelampur, clearance of, 43

Shafi, S.A., deposition before Shah Commission, 91, 92

Shahjada Bagh, clearance of, 43

Shankaran, R., as Commissioner in DDA, 42

Shankaran, V.C., 97

Sharma, K.N., 87

Shastri, Bhola Paswan, 40

Sheikh Sarai, clearance of, 43

Shekhar, Chandra, and VIP Land Grab Scandal, 99

Shukla, V.C., 115

Singh, Santokh, arrest during the Yamuna Bazar Clearance Operation, 34

Singh, Shoba, 173

Singh, Ranbir, 116, 117

Slum Areas (Improvement and Clearance) Act, 1956, 45, 123, 124, 128, 142, 143

Squatters/Slum-dwellers, commercial interests, exposure of, 38; during emergency, 45-48; features of, 19-20; four categories during and before the emergency, 58-59; gap between law and reality, 20; haphazard and ill-planned conditions of, 12, 13; meaning of, 20; Mrs Gandhi's observation about, 54-55; over-politicization of, 55; problems of, 75; study group recommendations for, 28-30; sub-human conditions of, 12, 13

Squatter Resettlement Scheme (1960), approval of, 27; features of, 27; Baleshwar Prasad's report on its transfer to DDA,

130-32; implementation of, 27, 28; problems of, 27, 28; revision of, 28
Squatter Resettlement Scheme (1975-1976), DDA contribution to, 48-54; *see also* Resettlement Colonies
Srivastava, K.K., 98
Srivastava, S.P., 135, 140
Srivastava, U.S., 84

Tamta, B.R., 46, 104; deposition before Shah Commission, 86, 87
Thatcher, Mrs Margaret, views on Delhi's progress, 16
Tilak Bridge, clearance of, 37
Turkman Gate, historical background of, 121
Turkman Gate Clearance Operation/Delhi-Ajmeri Gate Scheme, 18; average size of population in, 128; allotment of alternative plots, 162; analysis of, 168-69; background of, 122-28; bulldozers, use of, 127, 155, 156; causes of delay in the implementation of, 124, 125, 159, 160; DDA's Town Planners's Report (1975), 142; Delhi Improvement Trust Resolution of 1938, 122, 123, 128, 162, 163; Delhi Municipal Corporation Resolution of 1969, 136; deployment of police, 151-58; Draft Zonal Plan, 130; evidence before Shah Commission, 5, 6, 88-89; justification for taking up of, 131, 132; Land Acquisition Notification, 123, 159; liberal allotment procedure, 151; location and priority, 133; number of houses cleared, 122, 163; number of families involved, 134-36; procedures adopted, 126, 127, 133-37; story in *Indian Express*, 2, 3; unhealthy conditions in, 123, 126, 128 130
Turkman Gate incident, 169; Ashok Pradhan's evidence before Shah Commission, 148-49; CID (Special Branch) reports on, 144; concocted stories about, 77-83; curfew, 158; deployment of police force, 127, 149, 150; factors of, 144-57; firing, 127; riots, 126, 127, 146, 147, 149
Two Faces of Indira Gandhi by Uma Vasudev, concocted story in, 77

Unauthorized encroachment, after the emergency, 110, 111; demand for the use of DIR or MISA, 41, 42; increase of, 40
Urban land policy, 176

Vajpayee, A.B., and VIP Land Grab Scandal, 99
Vats, R.M., 101
Verghese, George, on the development of Ninth Delhi, 179
VIP Land Grab Scandal, Justice Debabratta Mukerjee's verdict on, 99; story of, 97-99; Supreme Court on, 98
Vishwanathan, 32, 174

Ward, Barbara, 177
World Bank, study of five typical cities of developing countries, 23

Yamuna Bazar Clearance Operation (1967-1968), background of, 31; Dr A.N. Jha's role in, 31-34; debate in Parliament on, 35; Congress and Jana Sangh on, 34; Press reactions, 35, 36